THE SPIRITUAL BREATHS

Breathing Exercises and Affirmations
that transform your life

This coursebook is based on *Brahma Vidya – An Ancient System of Yoga and Philosophy* by Swami K. S. Ramanathan, and Lectures given by Justice M. L. Dudhat

Santosh Sachdeva

YogiImpressions®

YogiImpressions®
THE EIGHT SPIRITUAL BREATHS
First published in India in 2012 by
Yogi Impressions Books Pvt. Ltd.
1711, Centre 1, World Trade Centre,
Cuffe Parade, Mumbai 400 005, India.
Website: www.yogiimpressions.com

First Edition, March 2012

Text and Illustrations copyright
© 2010 by Santosh Sachdeva

Cover design: Shivdutt Sharma
Illustration of exercises: Prabhakar Wairkar

Illustrations from *The Kundalini Trilogy (Conscious Flight Into The Empyrean, Kundalini Diary* and *Kundalini Awakening)* used with permission from Yogi Impressions

All rights reserved. This book may not be reproduced in whole or in part, or transmitted in any form, without written permission from the publisher, except by a reviewer who may quote brief passages in a review; nor may any part of this book be reproduced, stored in a retrieval system, or transmitted in any form or by any means electronic, mechanical, photocopying, recording, or other, without written permission from the publisher.

The information contained in this book is not intended to serve as a replacement for professional medical advice. Any use of the information in this book is at the reader's discretion. The author specifically disclaims any implied warranties of merchantability and fitness for a particular purpose and all liability arising directly or indirectly from the use or application of any information contained in this book. The author does not recommend the self-management of health or mental health problems. You should never disregard medical advice, or delay in seeking it, because of something you have learned in this book.

Printed at: Repro India Ltd., Mumbai

*This book is meant to serve as a beacon
for all aspirants who wish to
travel on the sacred path,
and for my children
Shibani, Nikki and Gautam.*

*"Salutations to that noble Guru
who by bestowing the knowledge of the Self
burns up the bondage created by
accumulated actions of innumerable births."*

– Guru Stotram

Swami K. S. Ramanathan
31.7.1922 – 19.3.2004

Swami K. S. Ramanathan was born in Thrissur, the cultural capital of Kerala. In 1985, he founded the 'Brahma Vidya Mission', in Mumbai. Brahma Vidya is the teaching which leads to the knowledge of the Brahman or the universe. The core of this teaching is contained in the Aitareya Upanishad. In the light of the knowledge that Brahma Vidya bestows upon earnest seekers – all doubt and disillusionment is removed from the mind. What comes shining through is eternal bliss and an everlasting peace. Many of the disciples who studied the teachings contained in Brahma Vidya and gained insights into it by practising the simple yoga exercises taught by him are, today in turn, spreading the light of Brahma Vidya among their followers.

Justice M. L. Dudhat
11.3.1935 – 22.9.2006

Justice M. L. Dudhat was born in Ahmednagar and completed his college education in Mumbai. He started his legal practice in the Bombay High Court in 1961. A meeting with Swami Ramanathan in 1979 led him to do the three-year course in Brahma Vidya. In 1985 Justice Dudhat started to spread the knowledge of Brahma Vidya by conducting classes at different locations in Mumbai. He followed the long tradition of householder Gurus, people who have gracefully borne the mantle of spiritual service while fulfilling the claims of a family and occupation.

Contents

Acknowledgements ... xiii
Preface ... xv

The Brimming Cup of Tea ... xvii
Origins of Brahma Vidya ... xix
Traditions of Spiritual Practice ... xxi

1
Chakras: The Energy Transformers ... 1

2
Kundalini Shakti ... 6

3
Signs of the Awakening Kundalini ... 13

4
Empowering the Mind ... 16

5
Prana and Pranayama ... 22

6
Pranayama: Preparation for the Breaths ... 30

7
The Breaths ... 34

8
Affirmations ... 38

9
The Memory Development Breath ... 41

10
The Revitalisation Breath ... 53

11
The Inspirational Breath ... 63

12
The Physical Perfection Breath ... 71

13
The Vibro-Magnetic Breath ... 77

14
The Cleansing Breath ... 87

15
The Grand Rejuvenation Breath ... 95

16
Your Own Spiritual Breath ... 103

17
Wisdom gained through the Breaths ... 108

18
A Healthy Mind in a Healthy Body ... 113

19
Thought Forms ... 117

20
Energy Blocks & Un-Ease ... 121

21
Preparation for Meditation ... 123

22
Meditation ... 129

23
Meditational Affirmations and Negations ... 132

24
Awakening ... 136

Books of Reference ... 139
Glossary ... 140

Acknowledgements

Firstly, I would like to pay my tribute to our family guru, Swami Mohangiriji, who is no longer on this plane, but is forever vigilant of my spiritual evolution. He saw the potential for my spiritual growth when he initiated me with a *Shiva mantra*, while I was a young girl.

My gratitude to the late Swami Ramanathanji, Founder of Brahma Vidya Mission, for his loving care and considering me a worthy recipient of the knowledge he imparted to me.

My love and regard for my Guru, the late Justice Dudhat, for encouraging me on the spiritual path; for his patience, continued support and guidance; for bringing peace, happiness and abundance into my life; and for awakening the creative spirit within me and my children.

To Shri C. S. Swaminathan, President of Brahma Vidya Mission, my gratitude for encouraging me to pursue the advanced course in Brahma Vidya.

I consider myself blessed for the encouragement and patience shown by my friend Nirmal Avi Almeida, while this book was still taking shape. I value her efforts in editing and synchronising the preliminary text and placing it in a logical order.

To Meera, for coming into my life at the perfect time and helping me determine the route I should take for this book. I treasure your friendship.

To Rohit Arya, for allowing me to tap into his vast knowledge and inherent wisdom.

To my brother, Shiv, for painstakingly editing and re-editing the books that I bring out. He has constantly been by my side through this journey.

To my son Gautam, for believing in the book and encouraging me to go deeper into the knowledge I had gained, in order for it to be a meaningful guide for all aspirants.

To my daughters Shibani and Nikki, for their unfailing belief in me and their constant moral support over the years.

To Prabhakar Wairkar, for his skilful illustrations delineating the postures for each of the Eight Breaths.

To Girish Jathar and Sanjay Malandkar for their painstaking DTP work to give the book its final form.

Finally, I take this opportunity to express my love and gratitude to all those who have contributed to my growth through special acts of love, generosity, friendship and kindness over the years.

Preface

Until recently, Brahma Vidya was taught as a course in self-development. It was designed to help aspirants access their unlimited inner potential. The intention being to work towards a positive, more desirable change within: one that would give access to higher knowledge and also fill one with peace, wisdom and compassion – all of which combine to transform human beings and make for a better world.

My own experience has clearly revealed that there is a lot more to human beings than the senses can feel or perceive. This course brings into your own direct experience and knowledge, the realisation that your ego is not your true being. Rather, your true being is the reality that never changes, and is not bound by time or space. It is immortal and self-existent. It always was, is, and ever will be. Since your true being is not bound by time or space, it cannot be grasped through the senses or the mind. It can only be experienced.

Human awareness is now making rapid breakthroughs in accessing new dimensions in consciousness. As Brahma Vidya is a science of evolution, it has to be kept updated and in harmony with the developing consciousness. To ensure this, Living Masters are sent at intervals to release the code in the 'practice'. The sages have said that, one who accepts tradition without independent personal thought does not perform any individual function in relation to human progress. He who accepts all the traditions of the past, subjects them to critical evaluation and adds the benefits of his own experiences, is the true propagator of light and an important factor in the higher evolution of mankind.

The basic Brahma Vidya course, under the guidance of Justice M. L. Dudhat, has evolved to a level hitherto not achieved. It has developed into a course that will lead an aspirant into the subtle planes of existence, if practised with awareness and understanding.

The breathing techniques are designed to activate the *chakras*, which will help an individual systematically access the descending and ascending energies of the *Kundalini*. This will, in turn, enable the aspirant to enter the experiential stage where knowledge is gained at the subtle level from subtle dimensions.

The Brimming Cup of Tea

A spiritual seeker who was eagerly in search of enlightenment and had performed many years of *sadhana* and study, now felt that he was ready for the final 'touch'. Thus, he went out in search of the guru who could grant him true enlightenment. Everyone told the man that high on top of a certain mountain lived an enlightened Master who could bestow enlightenment upon his disciples and devotees. The seeker travelled for weeks on foot to reach the Master in his cave at the top of the mountain. Upon arrival, he fell down at the Master's feet and proclaimed his earnest wish for enlightenment. The seeker proceeded to tell the Master of all the sadhana he had done, that which he had learned, that which he had experienced, and that which he felt he still needed to obtain.

The Master listened silently. When the seeker finally finished the long explanation of his own spiritual experiences, the Master said, "Let us have a cup of tea." The seeker looked shocked, "A cup of tea?" he exclaimed. "I've practised for years, meditated for years, searched for months, and walked for weeks in order to reach you so I could finally be granted enlightenment. I do not want a cup of tea. I want to be liberated!"

However, the Master calmly insisted that his visitor first have a cup of tea. The Master placed a cup on the ground, next to the seeker, and began to pour hot tea from the kettle into the cup. When the tea reached the brim of the cup, the Master did not stop pouring. Rather, he kept on pouring even as the tea began to flow over the sides of the cup, out of the saucer and on to the floor of the cave.

"Stop," the seeker cried. "The cup is full. It cannot hold any more. Please stop pouring the tea. It is all going to waste all over the floor."

The Master sat down and said to the seeker, "You are like this tea cup. You are so full of what you think you know, what you think you've achieved, what you think you've seen and what you think you need, that there is no room for me to teach you anything. Until you empty yourself of your own ego and your own illusions, my teaching will only go to waste like this tea on the floor."

Origins of Brahma Vidya

The origins of the ancient wisdom of the Spiritual Breaths are lost in time. The earliest recorded reference we have dates back to well over a thousand years.

At that time, the University of Nalanda was a world-renowned Buddhist centre of learning. Padmasambhava (730 AD – 805 AD), a great *tantric* and yogi, was then Head of the Department of Yoga and Philosophy. According to one of the numerous legends, he foresaw the destruction of Nalanda by foreign invaders and, along with his chosen students, migrated to Tibet. His sacred teachings were a closely guarded secret handed down over generations through his chosen disciples. Among these teachings was a set of powerful Breathing Exercises that had been designed to help human beings realise their highest potential. These Breathing Exercises were mastered by a spiritual seeker from the West, who was studying at the monastery in Tibet. He later returned to his country and created a course based on them. This he taught to his students, and also to spiritual aspirants through a correspondence course.

In Mumbai, K. S. Ramanathan completed this correspondence course and received permission to conduct it here. He called it the Brahma Vidya/Initiate Group Course and founded the Brahma Vidya Institute. This course was imparted in Mumbai through lectures, as well as a correspondence course to all those who were eager to imbibe the knowledge.

The Brahma Vidya course consists of Eight Breathing Exercises and their respective Affirmations. They start with *Pranayama* and end with meditation. It is designed to awaken as Ramanathanji says, the knowledge about "What life is, what is the origin of life, and what the continuation of life is – what it is that causes it all." One of his earnest students was Justice M. L. Dudhat. After studying and practising the course for three years, Justice Dudhat started conducting the course independently from 1985, at different locations in Mumbai.

I studied the course under him, and my personal awakening and understanding came in the form of visual knowledge that is recorded in a series of three books written in the format of daily entries in a diary, which form *The Kundalini Trilogy*. The Trilogy illustrates the transformation that the body-mind organism goes through during the practise of the Breaths in order to access the highest Truth. It includes several of the visuals I saw during meditations that helped me gain a clearer and deeper understanding of who we are, and how we are responsible for the direction we give to our life.

Research has shown that we rarely use more than five percent of our potential. The practise of this course results in the enhancement of your creative potential, increased levels of calmness, attainment of robust health and higher energy levels. Your enhanced state of peace and calm help you achieve ambitious goals in an effortless manner. The course has been designed to provide you with the necessary steps you will need to achieve mastery of your life across all dimensions.

The course consists of:

(i) Pranayama
(ii) Eight Breathing Exercises
(iii) Affirmations
(iv) Meditation

Traditions of Spiritual Practice

In earlier times, various systems of philosophy and mysticism designed their practices in relation to the development of consciousness at that time. In these systems, the seeker had to spend a number of years to bring into balance the trinity of his physical, mental and emotional being. This was done in ashrams, away from the distractions of mundane life, through devotion, service, physical discipline and surrender to the guru. That has now changed, and the knowledge that was imparted to a select few is now being offered to humanity at large. This is because human consciousness has taken a quantum leap at this stage of our evolution. In order to assist a larger number of seekers on their path, the knowledge that was kept well-guarded, is now being manifested in several forms. My own experience of the knowledge revealed to me has been traced in a visual diary contained in *The Kundalini Trilogy*, that traces the functioning of the Kundalini in the process of transforming the human body, mind and intellect. If one is surrendered, committed and has faith, the universe sends forth the necessary Master and the teachings to help guide the aspirant on his path.

Osho tells us that the Master is a presence, and not a doer. The presence works as a catalytic agent. He is a clear channel and through his presence much happens. It all really depends on the aspirant. If he is receptive and dedicated, the unfolding occurs. If the aspirant makes an intention and wishes to receive guidance, persons in and around the aspirant's field will appear at every step to facilitate the aspirant's progress on the spiritual path.

If he is not receptive, he limits the unfolding of the process. It all depends on how open and surrendered he is to receive what is being directed towards him.

Your Sadhana – Daily Practice

Before the start of your daily practice, you need to invoke the presence of the Master whose teachings you resonate with and, after you finish, you need to express gratitude for the help and guidance you are receiving. If you do not have a Master or guru, you may invoke the presence of the deity you worship or even the presence of someone you respect very highly. The attitude of gratitude generates a very powerful energy field and has tremendous potential to also transform negative energy into positive energy. There is no situation big or small that cannot be healed through the power of gratitude.

Remember, in the beginning, even though you are not sensing it, help is coming anyway. Energy follows thought and all thought has a form. So please know that as soon as you invoke the presence of a Master, it is there. If any questions or apprehensions arise during the practice, you can relax and ask for guidance or clarification, and it will come.

It can come in any form: in a book, in a dialogue with a friend or as a sudden insight. Nothing is left unanswered. There might be a lag time, but the clarification can also be immediate. The whole idea is to remain confident, relaxed and surrendered in the knowledge that no matter what, you will be looked after. If any experience happens, you are not to get focused on it. Just as thoughts come and go, in the same way you are to let go of the experience. Don't get attached to the experience, because it will not resurface. It has come and gone. Attachment of any kind is contracting and restricts growth.

The book you are now holding in your hands has come to you at a time when you are ready to take the challenge and responsibility for your own growth; a time when the human

Traditions of Spiritual Practice

consciousness has developed to an extent where it is equipped to hasten the process of its evolution and self-actualisation.

What is required of the seeker is clarity of intention, commitment, dedication and surrender. If you are surrendered, you are then taken care of and guided by your higher Self and the ascended Masters. If you have a Master or you are already in a programme of Pranayama and yoga, so much the better for you.

No life changes are required as such. You can go on with your daily living and family responsibilities. There is no restriction on diet; only indulgence needs to be avoided in all areas. You need to have a fixed place and time for your practice because you are creating a vibration in that place, which will support you. Also, the guidance that is directed towards you will be flowing at that particular time. If your routine is fragmented, the result will also be fragmented. There will not be an organised growth pattern. You need to follow the same rules that you would follow in a class. Just bear in mind that the more fragmented your practice, the more fragmented the result or, rather, no result at all. If you are not a dedicated student, the Masters are not going to be interested; they have other serious aspirants who need their attention. It is not a game you are playing, it is serious study.

When I went into the practise of the programme, I had put forth a very clear intention. It was, to know: "Who am I?" "Where do I come from?" And, "Where am I going?"

Once my intention was in place, I earnestly got into the routine of following the set programme. It consisted of scientific, spiritual Breathing Exercises, beginning with Pranayama and lessons in meditation. The Breaths activated the *Ajna* chakra so that I could observe the changes taking place in the mental, emotional and physical body.

The Eight Spiritual Breaths is intended to serve as a guide to aspirants and presents signposts to help them navigate their way on the spiritual path, and enable an increased understanding of who we are, and why we are here.

The Breathing Exercises, Affirmations and Meditations given here will help seekers gain a deeper understanding about the process of spiritual evolution and what it entails. This book also endeavours to clear any misconceptions and various kinds of fears that are associated with the process.

The Masters are doing their work on a massive scale, and at the rate human consciousness is expanding, it is now all the more important that we lend a hand not only by following and putting into practice what they are emphasising, but also by sharing this deeper understanding with more and more aspirants as we progress on the path.

At this point, I would like to share with you an anecdote about The Buddha which I have heard over the years. The disciples of Buddha, when they heard that their Master was ailing and only had a few more hours left to be in the physical form, went to pay homage to their Master and be with him in his final hours. The Buddha is known to have told his disciples: "It is very nice and good of you to have come to pay your homage to your Master and be with him in his final hours. But what would have been even better is that you would have continued with your practice."

Chapter One

Chakras: The Energy Transformers

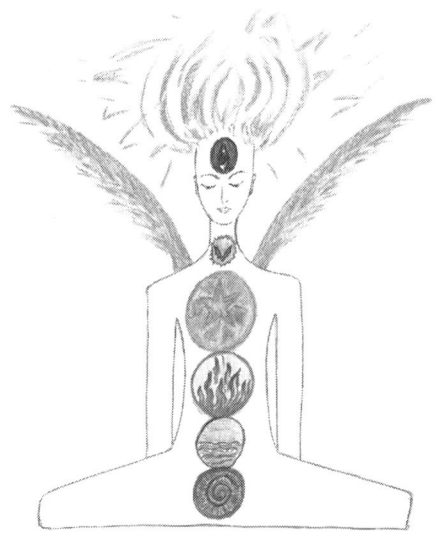

This visual does not depict the traditional chakras, but renders the chakras the way I visualised them.

According to seers, chakras are part of the etheric or subtle body and cannot be seen by the physical eye. The etheric body is an extensive network of energy channels, and at the points where these channels cross each other, they form a plexus or centre of energy. In Sanskrit, these intricate channels of energy are known as *nadis* (subtle channels) and the points where they intersect are known as chakras. Where only a few channels intersect each other, minor chakras are formed; where great streams of energy meet and cross, they form major chakras. The condition of a chakra has a definite influence on the endocrine glands. The chakras are very subtle and high-powered vortices of energy which receive the cosmic energy. They act as transformers to regulate the force of that energy so it may be used by the different organs in the physical body.

There are seven main chakras, though the seventh is not really a chakra and is termed as a centre because there is no plexus. Each of the six main chakras has its counterpart in the physical body in the form of vital organs (endocrine glands) and vitalises the area around it in the physical body. The health of an organ is dependent on the condition of the associated chakra. The more congested a chakra, the denser the related organ. Congestion of the chakra is related to the physical, mental and emotional baggage an individual body-mind organism carries throughout its evolution. Therefore, the chakras not only control and energise the physical body but also control and affect the individual's emotional and mental body.

The chakra can change its size, shape and movement according to the situation or emotion. The movement can change from rhythmic to chaotic. It can move like a flipped coin, clockwise or anti-clockwise, up and down like a coin on edge, or left-right like the pendulum of a clock. The rhythm changes according to the circumstance, situation or mood. The rhythm and vibration of the chakra also indicates whether the event is related to a person, place, or thing. It is through their highly developed and sensitive chakras that advanced aspirants can foretell the detail of an event that is to occur, or the identity of a person approaching them.

Varied movements of the Anahat chakra.

Chakras: The Energy Transformers

"Awakening of the chakras is a very important event in human evolution. It should not be misunderstood for mysticism or occultism, because with the awakening of the chakras, our consciousness and our mind undergo changes. These changes have significant relevance and relationship with our day-to-day life... The higher qualities of love, compassion, charity, mercy and so on are the expressions of a mind which is influenced by awakened chakras."

– Swami Satyananda Saraswati

It is contemplated that physical energy can be transformed into subtle energy through the actions of the chakras, and that the physical energy can be converted into mental energy within the physical dimension. As the chakras are activated and awakened, man becomes aware of the higher realms of existence, and also gains the power to enter those realms.

The Breathing Exercises that you will be practising, work at activating the chakras. It is essential that the chakras work in synchronicity so that the energy can flow freely. The chakras are vortices of psychic energy and their rhythm of vibration is determined by our feelings, emotions, and thought patterns.

The chakras

1. Sahasrar chakra (Crown Centre)
2. Ajna chakra (Brow or Third Eye)
3. Vishuddhi chakra (Throat)
4. Anahat chakra (Heart)
5. Manipur chakra (Navel)
6. Swadhisthan chakra (Sacral)
7. Muladhar chakra (Base)

When the *Sahasrar* centre opens, then a new consciousness dawns. Our present consciousness is not independent because the mind depends on information supplied by the senses. However, when the super-consciousness emerges, experience and knowledge become completely independent. The help of sense organs such as ears, eyes, nose etc. are not required. We see and sense what the physical eyes cannot see, hear the sounds which the ears cannot hear, smell the fragrance which the nose cannot smell, and feel the warmth of an embrace that nothing can match.

I present this vast knowledge in as precise and complete a structure as possible. I hope it helps all aspirants to understand the functioning of the body-mind organism. The best way is to approach every task in life with a playful attitude, finding humour and lightness in all situations instead of gnashing our teeth. Humour can lift us over the biggest stumbling blocks. A state of constant cheerfulness and always expecting the best leads us to new adventures and fulfillment. "What I sow, so shall I reap" – that is the Cosmic Law.

Endocrine glands

It is said that you are as old as your glands. If a young person feels old and weak, it is the glands that are responsible. If you feel vibrant, fully alive and energetic, it is the glands that are responsible. If you are depressed or enthusiastic in all that you think and do, it is the glands that are responsible. In fact, your health depends on the normal function or malfunction of one or more glands.

Each chakra exerts an influence on its related glands, e.g. the *Vishuddhi* chakra controls the para thyroid, thyroid and thymus glands. What influences the healthy/unhealthy functioning of the chakras and glands? It is your negative thoughts that overload the glands and cause them to become sluggish, weak and incapable of carrying out work of repair and maintenance.

Your glands can be recharged and stimulated medically, or you can recharge them through the practise of the breathing exercises given in this book along with their affirmations, and by your positively focussed thoughts.

Chakras: The Energy Transformers

Endocrine glands

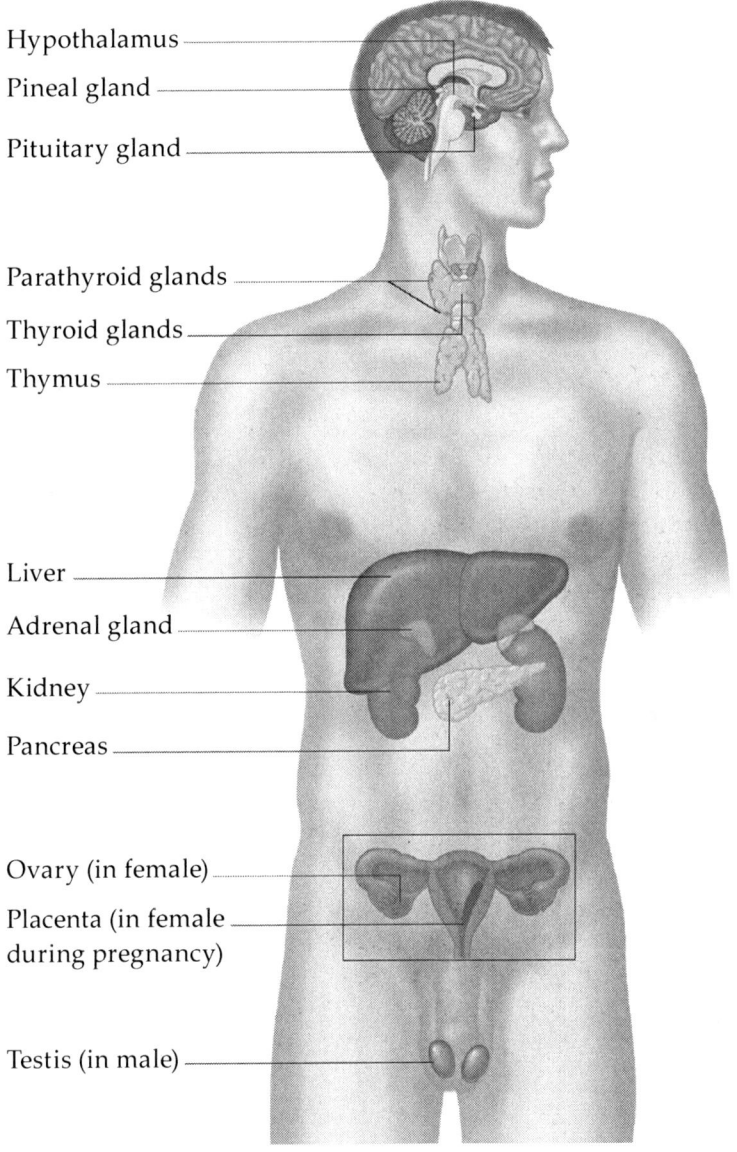

- Hypothalamus
- Pineal gland
- Pituitary gland
- Parathyroid glands
- Thyroid glands
- Thymus
- Liver
- Adrenal gland
- Kidney
- Pancreas
- Ovary (in female)
- Placenta (in female during pregnancy)
- Testis (in male)

Diagram showing the location of glands.

Chapter Two

Kundalini Shakti

What is Kundalini Shakti?

"Prana is both macrocosmic and microcosmic and is the substratum of all life. Mahaprana (the great prana) is the cosmic, universal, all-encompassing energy out of which we draw substance through the breathing process... The cosmic manifestation of prana or mahaprana in the individual body is represented by kundalini."

– Swami Niranjanananda Saraswati

Kundalini as Descending Energy

Invariably, when one reads about Kundalini, one reads about the ascent of Kundalini. The course of the Breathing Exercises and Affirmations that you will be practising follow the path of the Descending Energy and we term it as the Descent of Kundalini. The force descends first to the head, then to the

The stimulus of Kundalini produces fields of symmetrical shape in the brain hemispheres.

heart, then to the navel, and then lower. In other words, entering the Sahasrar centre, it moves into the *Ajna* chakra, then into the Vishuddhi chakra, into the *Anahat* chakra, then into the *Manipur* chakra and the other chakras down the line. This is the safe path. Kundalini, the descending force, moves into the brain where it influences the negative and positive polarities or the left and right brain hemispheres, dispelling dullness and passivity.

As the Kundalini moves down through the chakras, it activates and opens them, making our talents a useful part of our life and awakening us to our potential. It is bringing the awareness of God-consciousness into our lives.

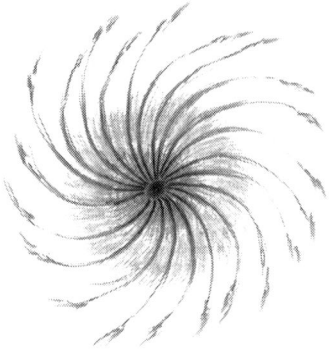

An awakened and active chakra.

"When the descent of Kundalini occurs, it means the lower mental plane of the aspirant is no longer influenced by the ordinary mind, the super mind takes over instead. This higher form of consciousness rules the body, mind and the senses and directs your life, thoughts and emotions. Kundalini is henceforth the ruler of your life. That is the concept of descent."
– Swami Satyananda Saraswati

"Sri Aurobindo says that 'unless there is descent of the light that permeates not only the mind, but also becomes an all-powerful force touching and transforming the levels that are physical and below, no real transformation transpires'. Sri Aurobindo declares that even the descent of light is not sufficient. It must be the descent of whole consciousness and its manifestations such as peace, power, knowledge, love, ananda (bliss)."
– John White

The Eight Spiritual Breaths

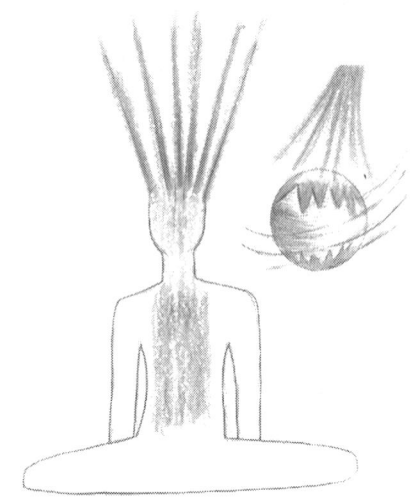

Descent of solar force into the physical plane.

Solar Force

One can say that Prana, or the solar force, interpenetrates all matter and acts perpetually on it. The unfoldment of your spiritual nature is just the manifestation of that vital energy derived from the Highest Light (the sun behind the sun) – the sun and its Divine Source – in you. This has been known to the sages as the solar force, proceeding from the Creator of the sun and the worlds.

The above visual shows how the solar energy or solar force descends to the physical plane. The magnetic solar rays strike the earth and break through the earth's crust to its very core, thus bringing the vegetable kingdom to life. This solar energy penetrates the seed, pushing its matter downwards as roots.

To understand the solar force, so that you can control and use it rightly, you must discover it in the realm of life and through the physical body.

Kundalini Shakti

Solar force activating the chakras and the Sahasrar centre.

The solar force manifests on the physical plane of our life by passing through a collection of nerve centres or chakras in the subtle body, and then up the spine to the brain. Here, its currents unite to build the spiritual body. The descending solar force penetrates the body and ascends by means of two channels running along the right and left sides of the spine. The channel on the left is the *Ida* nadi, and the one on the right is the *Pingala* nadi. Ida conducts the consciousness and Pingala conducts the life force. These two nadis feed the two hemispheres of the brain which in turn control every activity of the body. The endeavour ultimately is that the solar force moves up the central channel known as the *Sushumna* nadi (the subtle channel in the spinal cord). This solar force activates the chakras or centres as it moves through them. These chakras concentrate the fire of the solar force. In the cerebro-spinal system there are many centres awaiting regeneration and this is achieved through right breathing. This effect is first felt and recognised on the physical plane when we express greater physical well-being; and, secondly, on the mental plane when we are happier and more energetic; and, thirdly, on the spiritual plane, when we see that we are more peaceful by virtue of greater knowledge of the Law of the Universe.

With the descent of Kundalini we bring down to the physical plane a transformed consciousness. We live a normal life, going through its ups and downs, highs and lows, losses and gains, attachments and infatuations; in fact we go through all the emotions in their negative and positive aspects without getting enmeshed in them.

Kundalini as the Ascending Energy

Kundalini *shakti* (energy) is the name given to the dormant force lying at the root of the spine. In its unmanifested state, it is symbolised as a serpent coiled in three-and-a-half circles. When it is ready to awaken and unfold, it ascends up the Sushumna passing through the chakras, starting with the Muladhar, Swadhisthan, Manipur, Anahat, Vishuddhi and Ajna chakras and up to the Sahasrar centre where it unites with pure-consciousness.

The Ascending Kundalini.

How does the Kundalini shakti awaken? It is awakened in two stages: first, it can awaken naturally, and second, by awakening it under the guidance of a Master. The awakening could be experienced as a sudden, intense, mind-blowing experience. Such an experience is rare. Usually bursts of this energy are released as bursts of enthusiasm, peak experiences or a sense of well-being.

The awakening as an explosive experience.

In its awakened state, the Kundalini has been visualised in its different aspects by various aspirants. Given on the following page is a visual of the energy in its awakened state; as an emerald green snake moving up the spine, with a mouth like a flaming cauldron of fire throwing out tongues of flames.

Once the Kundalini has completed its work of purifying the body-mind organism, it moves as pure golden light, giving the feeling of a golden snake.

The Eight Spiritual Breaths

An aspect of the Ascending Kundalini. *Light body or golden snake.*

Kundalini and the chakras belong to the subtle body, while the physical body has organs that correspond to them. You may not feel the chakras; it is also not necessary that you will feel the Kundalini. If the passage is clear, the energy flows but you may not feel it; you will feel it when there is something that resists the flow.

When the Kundalini awakens, the physical body undergoes changes. Its cells become charged and rejuvenated with high energy and a process of complete transformation is set in motion. The Breathing Exercises are designed to purify the Ida, Pingala and Sushumna nadis, for when the Kundalini awakens there should be no resistance.

As far as my understanding and experience goes, I believe that the Breathing Exercises are designed to prepare the body-mind intellect for the awakening.

The awakening of the Kundalini energy would of course depend upon the level of consciousness an aspirant has attained. It can happen with the practise of the first Breath, or it could take its own time. It would also depend on the level of commitment, determination and the intensity of desire.

Chapter Three

Signs of the Awakening Kundalini

"One of the most important things I learned from my own Tibetan teachers is that sacred traditions are built around the experiences of individual men and women who have had direct mystical experience of the spiritual path. I discovered that there were guides and teachers who were able to provide spiritual road maps, pointing out pitfalls as well as shortcuts. Experienced teachers can help seekers understand these maps and develop and grow along the path. We can learn from their experience, and they can inspire us along the way, and model how to live a beautiful, loving, and spiritual life. Today, there are many authentic spiritual teachers who walk their talk and live in the truth. It's not just something that Jesus did or the Dalai Lama does."

– Lama Surya Das

Knowledge about the ascending Kundalini differs from person to person. For example, it is not necessary that my experiences or the visuals given in my earlier books will correspond with yours, if you are going through a visual experience in your meditation. In general, the content of the mystical experiences and the symbols visualised will reflect the religious and cultural background of the aspirant who is going through the experience: a Hindu will tend to see visions of *Shiva* or his chosen deity, a Christian will see visions of Mary or Christ, and a Native American may see visions of animals and birds such as sacred crows, buffaloes or wolves. A Hindu may get a symbol of a trident, a Christian may see a cross, a Zoroastrian may see a symbol of fire, a Native American may see a feathered headgear and so on. The symbols have their own language and point towards a person's lineage and history.

When Kundalini follows the descending path and moves down towards the physical plane, it transforms the consciousness. You live a normal life fulfilling your duties and obligations towards family and friends, like anyone else. You may go through the play of desires, passions and cravings. You may go through infatuation and attachment, but you are going through it with awareness. You are not involved in it with your heart and soul. It is like an actor playing a role. This is possible because all the data that is released by the lower three chakras is now dealt with awareness, understanding and dispassion.

In the course of your practice there may be an isolated awakening in the Ajna chakra, in which case awareness enters the realms of the unconscious and you may see weird figures, entities, monsters or benevolent beings. You may hear and see many things that are inexplicable. There is no reason to be startled or confused. Understand that all these are the products of your unconscious mind. The data stored in your unconscious, related to your beliefs, fears and fantasies now surfaces. You need to ignore it because it is not tangible and can do no harm. Just watch, observe and let it go.

You may hear *nada* (mystical sounds). This is a sign of purification of the nadis due to Pranayama. This is a subtle sound where the ear i.e. the aural faculty is not involved. You may hear a constant *chinnnnn* sound, something like the sound made by crickets. There can be a sound of a bell, conch, lute, drum, strong breeze or rumbling clouds or thunder, and lastly, you may hear the echo or *hmmm* of the beaten drum. These sounds emanate from the Anahat chakra and are due to the vibrations of *Prana* in the heart.

Various kinds of lights may manifest in white, yellow, red, blue, green or misty colours, or they may appear like flashes of lightning and burning coals. The appearance of lights mean that you are transcending physical consciousness.

If your eyes start to roll, your tongue turns and slides back or its tip touches your palate; if your teeth start clicking or you start shaking, do not worry as these are all signs of the awakening Kundalini. Carry on with your routine practice without fear, as it is all a part of purification and transformation.

Signs of the Awakening Kundalini

You may feel you are being attacked, but it is only a feeling. If you are clear within yourself and understand the phenomenon, it will just pass off. You may feel that you are being poked and prodded; or, you may feel a burning or a cooling sensation. If you stay relaxed, you make it easy for yourself and also for the energy to do its work. You might feel pain around the eyes or forehead or pressure against the third eye area; there is no need to worry. It is caused by restrictions in the related meridians. In due course, the meridians in this area will dilate and the flow of energy will be smoother.

You may experience jerks, at times violent ones, in your physical body. Remember that Kundalini is subtle body energy. When it is moving through the constricted, subtle body meridians, the subtle body goes through a spasm that is felt as a jerk in the physical body. If you get locked in a posture, just be an observer – it will unlock by itself. Don't forget that you have entered the programme of transformation and in order to do that the Creative Intelligence within you is going through an intricate process of recreating you. It knows exactly what it is doing and is aware of your level of tolerance. You can make it comfortable for yourself by surrendering unreservedly to the awakened Kundalini. This surrender is the unconditional surrender of a vibrant, conscious individual and not a dull, lifeless surrender.

It is very important to be honest and diligent in one's practice for if the Kundalini awakens prematurely, it can create problems in any one of the chakras by multiplying the force of the behaviour associated with that chakra. If one has unfulfilled desires and negative tendencies, premature awakening will enhance these tremendously.

If you become fearful, then the right thing to do is to stop and go back to your old way of life till you have a better understanding and are more balanced in your mental, emotional and physical body. When you feel ready, you can start again.

Chapter Four

Empowering the Mind

Time and again, emphasis is laid on breath and its importance. You will be reminded of this, again and again, until it seeps into your subconscious and breathing correctly becomes a way of life with you. Life, itself, depends upon breath; everything in nature pulsates to its rhythm. We human beings can live a comparatively longer time without food, a shorter time without water, but without breathing we can only last a very, very, short time. The benefits of correct breathing cannot be explained in words, they have to be experienced. When someone asked the author of *The Power of Now*, Eckhart Tolle's advice as to which course he should do from a vast number of courses being offered in a brochure of a spiritual organisation, Eckhart's answer was, "They all look so interesting. But I do know this, be aware of your breathing as often as you are able, whenever you remember. Do this for one year, and it will be more powerfully transformative than attending all of these courses. And it's free... One conscious breath is enough to make some space where before there was uninterrupted succession of one thought after another."

On the subject of Meditation, you will observe that the initial lessons and affirmations are guiding you to develop the ability of rejuvenation to help you to live a long and healthy life. If we cannot control our bodies so as to command good health as long as we desire, then we cannot fully realise our highest hopes. Therefore, do not question, do not doubt. Everything will become clear as you continue with the practice.

I embarked on the course with the clear intention of knowing the 'origin of my source' and, I can categorically state, that is what I got to know. The course follows the simple rule of 'Seek and you shall find. Ask and it shall be given unto you.' This will happen if you actually get into the practice, rather than gain a mere intellectual understanding of it. The desire to know, and the urge to achieve your goal, has to be strong and you must be convinced you will achieve it.

In the process of living, we first think, then feel, and thirdly, we act. Because you feel, you know it is possible. This conviction must be firmly rooted in your mind and then passed on to the sphere of feeling. You must know that you feel it. You are alive with the feeling of it – it is burning itself into your consciousness. Because your whole being is alive with the truth that you feel, you will make of your life exactly what you want it to be. Without this clear conviction – unshakeable and fully established – that you can do what you truly desire to do, achieve whatever you want to achieve – it is not possible to move ahead. Therefore, practise the following exercise with feeling:

Close your eyes and think: "I am the Master of my own life! I will do what I desire to do." Now say this loudly and say it several times. Then rest. Now say it again with more feeling... say it as if you know you are the Master of your own life, for no one else is. Say, "I rejoice – I did not feel this before, but now I know it! I feel with all the power of my being that I am the Master of my own life – and I will truly begin to live it."

Not only must the mind see, and the consciousness feel the certainty, but the conviction still has to pass into the imagination that "I am the Master of my own life – and I will truly begin to live it" or anything else that you desire. Imagination is the creative faculty of every individual. It is this faculty that causes us to do what we do. Your imagination is the creative faculty of the Infinite, which dwells within. None of us can do anything without the idea of it first coming to us through our own imaginative and creative faculty.

Although the imagination is your own creative faculty, you have to learn what to do with it, how to control and direct it. If you do not direct it, it will direct you. Remember, the creative faculty will do for you whatever you train it to do.

If you do not direct it, it directs you according to the traditions of your culture and of your beliefs, including the negative beliefs of failure, disappointment, disease, death and decay. Now, you are a part of a culture and a belief system, and when you accept its traditions and beliefs without question, you cannot escape the results of those beliefs and traditions.

Recitation:

"I am the Master of my own life! I will do what I desire to do."
"I am the Master of my own life! I will do what I desire to do."
"I am the Master of my own life! I will do what I desire to do."
"I rejoice – I did not feel this before, but now I know it! I feel with all the power of my being that I am the Master of my own life – and I will truly begin to live it."

Mind

All that we know is made known to us through thought. We have to think with something. In other words, we have to have a substance with which to think – and that substance is 'mind'. There must be an embodiment through which the Spirit or Life must express itself. Some embodiments can be seen and felt, while there are others that are subtle and cannot be seen or felt. Mind is one of the subtle substances that cannot be seen or felt. The product of the unseen substance we call 'mind' is 'thought', which also is subtle unless expressed in word or form.

All thoughts are released as soon as the mind creates them. Bring a thought into manifestation within the mind and you simultaneously manifest it through the universe... as in the microcosm, so also in the macrocosm. This is the law of creation. Just as you store thoughts as beliefs in the subconscious, so also those thoughts/beliefs are stored in the collective unconscious. As we go through life, we create stories about ourselves as to who we are and how the world should be in relation to us. We create our own story line and bring in irrational beliefs or words like 'ought', 'should' and 'must', instead of viewing a situation as 'is'. "My belief makes me believe that it is the only right belief. If it is okay for me to be in a certain way, it should be okay for you, too," not realising that the other person has her own story line and probably her own belief system in place. How can the erroneous thoughts/beliefs be replaced? They cannot be erased to make them disappear. The only way is by transforming them and this is accomplished when the two polarities (the right and left brain) balance each other in the unconscious.

Reason and Imagination

There should be no conflict between reason and imagination. You should not mistake one for the other, as they are totally different faculties.

Reason

Reason does not create – it cannot. The imagination creates – that is all it can do and does. The reasoning faculty reasons, takes decisions, and its work ends there. The imagination does not reason – it can't. Therefore, when reason says "I want to grow young and remain young, but I am afraid that I won't," the 'I won't' is an instruction to the imagination in line with the belief system. That thought of 'I won't' creates negative conditions, and so your desire ends there. Therefore, let reason be convinced that it is possible for you to think and breathe yourself back to youth.

'Thought' is the strongest power in the world. Thought is the prime cause of life. Movement and action are the effect of that cause.

Imagination

Your imagination is the miracle-worker of your life. You know that you are what you think or the way you imagine yourself to be. The image you see in the mirror is what you imagine yourself to be in appearance. Imagination is the faculty of the Creator within you. You are what you think you are. The moment you change your thought, you change. Your imagination is that faculty within you that paints the pictures, that presents the images, that inspires you with the most fascinating ideas of what you can do. But, imagination cannot reason, it is non-reasoning, and is not subject to reason.

Therefore, when imagination, with the fascination of an unseen artist, creeps into your mind with all sorts of schemes, hopes and desires, pictures and images, and whispers to you that you can be a great man or woman; tells you that you can do something that has never been done before; tells you that whatever you are doing, you can do that much better than you are now doing it; tells you that you can be healthy and well and happy, that you can make more money; that you can become the greatest person that ever lived in your particular sphere of activity... what happens? You are thrilled. All this goes on in your mind and you are intensely happy. Things around you mean nothing when you are in that state. You exult. You see yourself triumphant. You are the conqueror. You are the optimist. You are alive with hope and you are very happy. So, the world floats by while you are enjoying your serenity and achievement. You feel that you can be well... can do more... and be more... can live as long as you desire. You are getting the message – "You can *be* what you want to be, and you can *do* what you want to do."

Now, after all this, when you say, "Yes, I feel that I can be more than I am, but I know that I won't," all the beautiful work the imagination has done, crumbles. The 'I won't' is an instruction to the imagination confirming the belief to create negative conditions, so your desires go up in smoke. Therefore, let there be no conflict in the mind between reason and imagination.

Empowering the Mind

In the science of these Breaths and their related Affirmations, what is emphasised in the first few chapters is the need for building in our consciousness, the irrevocable idea of life – life – life! You and I are life, and life is eternal. We emphasise the need for building into our consciousness, the belief that you and I should have the divine privilege of exercising our inherent power to live. There is a power within us which, when we fully understand it, we should be able to control. And, it should render us immune from those conditions that cause disease, disharmony and imbalance on every plane of our existence.

Picture in your mind a person, full of life and vigour, energy and hope, and believe in the manifestation of Divine power within you of intense personal magnetism, that will enable you to direct human activities in line with your highest hopes. In short, a leader throbbing with power and attracting to yourself only that which is in unison with all that is good.

You must not say that you cannot make a fresh start.

You must not say you cannot do what you would like to do.

You must not say you lack anything whatever, to keep you from being whatever you want to be.

Believe that you can conquer and believe that strongly within you. Although you may not yet know it, there is a power that causes the universe to be what it is, and that power is within you, so you cause who and what you are.

Chapter Five

Prana and Pranayama

The free-flow of Prana moves in from the Manipur chakra and out through the Ajna chakra.

The sages have taught us that there is a substance in the air from which all life has emanated and that substance is Prana or life force. When we speak of Prana, we do not mean the breath, air or oxygen; it is the original life force. This life force is everywhere; it pervades all existence – animate and inanimate. As Prana is part of the air and atmosphere, we are constantly breathing it in. In the physical body, Prana is stored in the brain and nerve centres. The pathways of *pranic* currents which flow throughout the body are known as nadis. These are the subtle channels of energy in the pranic body. Nerves relate to the physical body, whereas nadis relate to the pranic, vital body and to the more subtle *koshas* or subtle bodies. Nadis provide energy through a vast communication network of fibre-like links carrying Prana back and forth in every direction.

According to yogic literature there are 72,000 nadis. Out of these 72,000 nadis, there are ten main nadis of which three are most important. These three nadis are the Ida, Pingala and Sushumna as the central channel. These three nadis originate from the *Muladhar* chakra, which is situated at the base of the spine. Generally, Prana is partially released from the Muladhar chakra, through the Ida and Pingala channels, which run alongside the spine crossing each other at the different chakras.

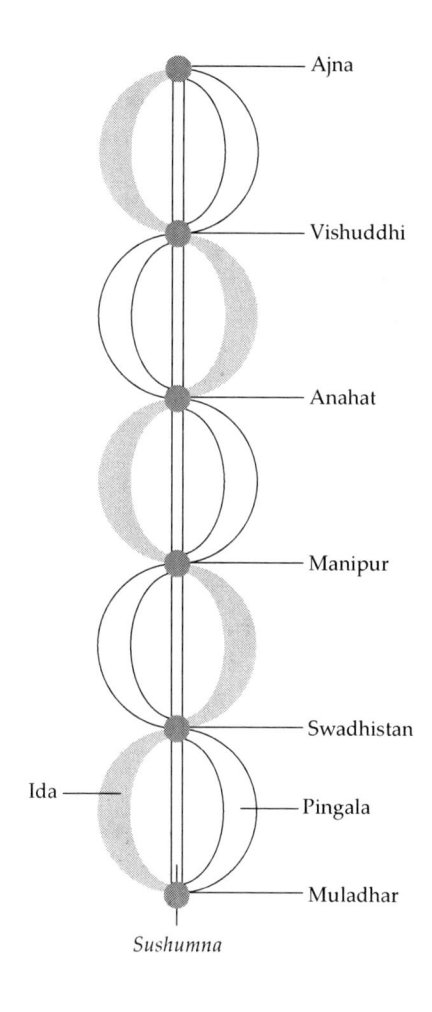

- Ajna
- Vishuddhi
- Anahat
- Manipur
- Swadhistan
- Ida
- Pingala
- Muladhar
- Sushumna

In Pranayama, we learn to manipulate the flow of Prana in different ways.

Ida is the channel for mental energy, Pingala is the channel for Prana shakti or solar energy. When the breath is flowing more through the right nostril, we say the Pingala is active and then one is more energetic and dynamic. When breath is flowing more through the left nostril, we say Ida is active. Ida is the conductor of *manas* shakti, the mental or lunar energy. When this nadi is flowing, then there may be a feeling of tranquillity, dreaminess or mental activity; it is a more passive energy. Sushumna nadi is for spiritual energy. When both nostrils are flowing, we say that Sushumna is active. Sushumna is the conductor of *Mahaprana*, the spiritual energy of Kundalini. When Sushumna is flowing, it is the most favourable time for any type of sadhana. During this phase a feeling of equanimity and a meditative state can arise spontaneously.

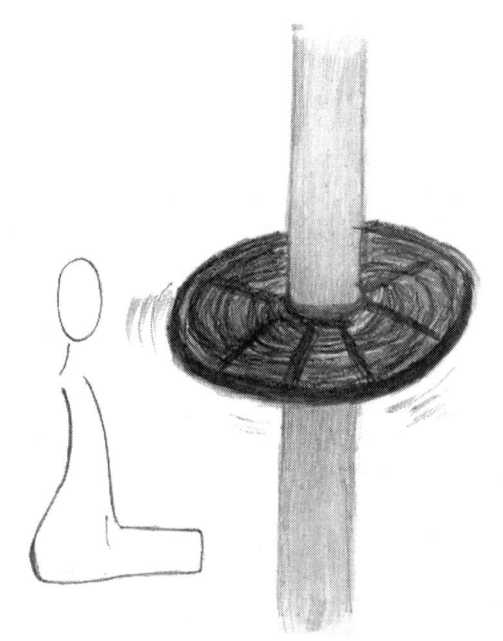

Magnified visual of Sushumna nadi with chakra rotating on it.

To sum up:

Pingala: With every inhalation through the right nostril, a positive current flows through the Pingala located on the right side of the spine. This is solar energy and creates heat in the body.

Ida: With every inhalation through the left nostril, a negative current flows through the Ida located on the left side of the spine. This is lunar energy and creates coolness in the body.

Sushumna: This is the central channel and is equivalent to the spine in the subtle body. This stands like a pillar tinged with gold. All nadis and chakras receive their power from it.

Just as the blood appropriates oxygen from the air and circulates it through the physical body, so Prana is carried to all parts of the nervous system adding strength and vitality to it. When you learn to breathe properly, you are taking in more of the vital force. The sages measure the span of human life not by the number of years they live, but by the number of breaths they take from the moment they are born until they die. Because the breath is the vehicle of Prana, they devised techniques of breathing that would enhance an individual's life and help him gain mastery over it.

Different aspects of Prana are realised through Pranayama. This is a breathing technique through which the quantity of Prana in the body is multiplied and its energy level enhanced. The science of Pranayama is based on breath-retention, with the result that nervous impulses are stopped in different parts of the body; brain-wave patterns are controlled and mental agitation is curtailed.

Prana, solar force or the life-giving principle, inter-penetrates all matter. Perpetually playing on matter, it causes different rates of vibration in the different densities. The more subtle the matter of any living thing – the less resistance is there to the cosmic force, and higher are the vibrations and the resultant consciousness. When an individual has mastered the flow of Prana, there will be an overall improvement in the function of all physical organs; he will experience clarity in his thinking process. He will develop greater awareness and ability to cope with situations, thus leading to an enhanced understanding of a definite purpose behind every thought, action and expression.

The five Pranas

"In order to control the function of the body, Prana shakti manifests as five major Prana vayus: Prana, Apana, Samana, Udana and Vyana. In the Upanishads, Prana vayu is also called the 'in breath'. Vyana is the 'all-pervasive breath'. Prana is inhalation; Apana, exhalation; Samana, the time between the two; and Udana, the extension of Samana. Each vayu is interdependent and interconnected."

– Swami Niranjanananda Saraswati

Prana the sub-prana called Prana belongs to the specific part of the body between the larynx and upper part of the diaphragm. It controls the activity of the heart and lungs.

Apana is located in the pelvic region between the navel and the perineum; it controls activities of the kidneys, bladder, bowels, the excretory and reproductive organs.

Samana is situated between the ribcage and the navel. It functions as a balance or equalizer between the two opposite forces of Prana and Apana. Samana controls and activates the digestive organs and the secretions they supply.

Udana is located in the arms, legs and head. It is responsible for all the sensory organs and the organs of action. It controls the sympathetic and parasympathetic nervous system.

Vyana is the vital force that pervades the whole body and acts as reserve energy. It helps and boosts all other pranas when required. It regulates and coordinates all the muscular movements and the other pranas.

The panch koshas

The panch koshas or five sheaths and the six chakras form the basis of the Kundalini shakti and the activity of this energy manifests in these sheaths. The five koshas are five sheaths that form the covering for the soul.

Anandamaya kosha
(Bliss)

Vijyanmaya kosha
(Higher Knowledge, Intuition)

Manomaya kosha
(Mind, Intellect, Memory Reasons)

Pranamaya kosha
(Vital Energy)

Annamaya kosha
(Food-body or Gross Body)

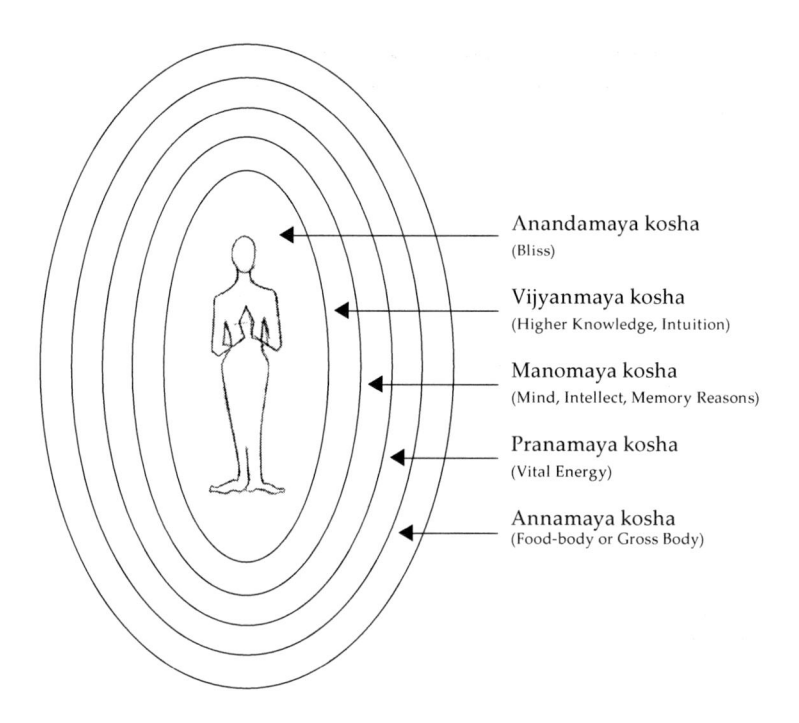

1. **Annamaya kosha (Sheath of Food)**
   The outermost sheath is the grossest of all and is in the form of the physical body. The development, stability and maintenance of this sheath depends upon *anna* (food). Hence it is called Annamaya kosha.

2. **Pranamaya kosha (Sheath of Prana, the overall Life Force)**
   Pranamaya kosha is a collection of five pranas (vital energies that comprise the Prana), namely Prana, Apana, Udana, Vyana and Samana. In the physical body, Prana, consisting of the five pranas, refers to that level of life force that provides movement and activity to the gross physical body and the sense organs that makes the body capable of functioning. In the absence of Prana, the gross physical body becomes lifeless. All the subtle senses exist in the Pranamaya kosha. Inhalation and exhalation is one of its activities.

3. **Manomaya kosha (Sheath of Mind)**
   The mind, intellect, ego and accumulated impressions form the Manomaya kosha. It is the regulator of both the Annamaya kosha and Pranamaya kosha. This sheath is the foundation of the conscious and subconscious mind and is the storehouse of good and bad impressions. The outward and inward flow of intellect depends on this sheath. The Manomaya kosha controls the senses through the medium of Pranamaya kosha. It is the function of the Pranamaya kosha to impart energy, agility and activity to the senses; but what to do or not to do is the function of the mind. The mind gives an order and the Prana becomes active through the senses.

4. **Vijnanamaya kosha (Sheath of Wisdom)**
   In this sheath, the intellect evolves to a point where it can grasp the essence of any subject.

5. **Anandamaya kosha (Sheath of Bliss)**
   It is the sheath of the eternal blissful nature of the *atma* or the Self.

"All these dimensions of being are interpenetrating and interacting... All our sadhana is directed at enabling us to develop awareness of all five of these sheaths and of the glorious atman beyond... Each sheath is composed of energy, energy vibrating at different speed. In the physical sheath, the energy vibration is at its slowest. As we move through the koshas the vibration becomes faster and finer until it once again resolves itself back into pure consciousness. For energy is but the dynamic form of consciousness and consciousness is potential form of energy."

– Swami Muktananda

The chakras and their related elements and koshas

1. Sahasrar chakra (Crown Centre) – is everything and nothing, it is the merging of consciousness and Prana. It is associated with Anandamaya kosha (bliss).

2. Ajna chakra (Brow or Third Eye) – associated with element manas (mind) and Vijanamaya kosha (higher knowledge, intuition).

3. Vishuddhi chakra (Throat) – associated with element ether and Vijanamaya kosha (higher knowledge, intuition).
4. Anahat chakra (Heart) – associated with element air and Manomaya kosha (mind, intellect, memory, reason).
5. Manipur chakra (Navel) – associated with element fire and Pranamaya kosha (vital energy).
6. Swadhisthan chakra (Sacral) – associated with element water and Pranamaya kosha (vital energy).
7. Muladhar chakra (Base) – associated with element earth and Annamaya kosha (food body or gross body).

Tattvas

Tattvas are the five components of the Mahaprana which is described as 'the life principle of the universe and of human beings'. In the Upanishads, Tattvas are referred to as the 'five vital elements' that compose the physical body. Each Tattva has its negative and positive phase and every thought and act excites a Tattvic vibration. Tattvas govern the body, physically, mentally, psychically and spiritually. Every nerve current is controlled by that Tattva, which is attributed to it.

The physical body is always in vibration with energy flowing in harmony, or in discord, in accordance with our power of control of the Tattvic element, which we acquire through the practise of Pranayama.

The five Tattvas (elements) are:

1. Akasha Tattva: most refined of the elements, directs the sense of hearing.
2. Vayu Tattva: element of air, directs the sense of touch.
3. Tejas Tattva: element of fire, directs the sense of sight.
4. Apas Tattva: element of water, directs the sense of taste.
5. Prithvi Tattva: element of earth, directs the sense of smell.

Chapter Six

Pranayama: Preparation for the Breaths

The practise of Pranayama is powerful. Please follow the instructions carefully.

Pranayama will help to bring into balance the positive and negative polarities or the right and the left brain hemispheres. The left brain is the logical brain and represents 'illusion'. The right brain is the creative brain and represents 'truth'. The left brain is comprised of the individual ego and the right brain represents the creative source.

Pranayama is to be practised for one week before starting on the Breathing Exercises. This is to be done daily before commencing the exercises. Pranayama prepares the body for the Breathing Exercises, therefore the emphasis on doing the practice for a week before commencing on Breath No. 1.

You should do two cycles of Pranayama four times during the day: morning, afternoon, evening and night, before going

Pranayama: Preparation for the Breaths

to bed. You can be sitting in your car waiting at the traffic light or at your office desk. Except in the morning, where you sit at the place you have assigned for your practice, Pranayama can be practised at any convenient time and place.

Before commencing, you need to relax. Sit cross-legged on a cushion or sit on a chair. Keep your spine absolutely erect and not leaning against any backrest. This is advised because the subtle body extends about two inches from your physical body. The chakras are in the subtle body and if you lean back or slouch, you are compressing the chakras and not allowing the free flow of energy. Close your eyes and take four or five deep breaths. With Pranayama we are attempting to clear the passages of the Ida, Pingala and Sushumna.

Visualisation for Pranayama

In this visual you see that while we are going through the Pranayama, the Prana we breathe in is light in colour, and the toxic Prana we breathe out is a shade darker in colour.

Inflow and outflow of Prana.

Posture for the practise of Pranayama

Fig. 1   Fig. 2   Fig. 3

Fig. 4   Fig. 5   Fig. 6

How to practise Pranayama

1. Sit in a cross-legged position, keep your spine absolutely straight or as straight as possible, without any strain, with no tension or pain anywhere. Those who are unable to sit in this position comfortably may sit on a chair (without leaning back against the back rest), or even stand if necessary. Put your right thumb lightly on your right nostril, your pointer finger and middle fingers should be placed lightly between the brows (Ajna chakra) and your ring or third finger on the left nostril.

2. With the right thumb, close the right nostril gently (without pressure). During inhalation, breathe in steadily (not too slowly) through the left nostril, counting up to four. Hold the breath (gently closing both nostrils) without any strain anywhere, and while doing so count to sixteen (mentally). Release the pressure on the right nostril. Exhale steadily through the right nostril while you count to eight.

Pranayama: Preparation for the Breaths

3. While still keeping your left nostril closed with the ring finger of the right hand, breathe steadily (not too slowly) through the right or positive nostril, counting up to four. Retain the breath by gently closing both nostrils, without any strain, and mentally count to sixteen. While lifting the ring finger to release the pressure on the left nostril, exhale through the left or negative nostril, as you count to eight; this is one cycle. You have to repeat this for two cycles. In case you find the count uncomfortable, you can adjust it to suit your convenience in the ratio 2:8:4. There should be no strain of any kind. There should be no violent inhalation or you might harm yourself.

Rings of the elements that compose the body encompass my form.

With correct breathing, we bring in the universal force that corresponds to the elements that compose the body. These elements are renewed with every breath and the more even and rhythmic the breathing, the more pranic energy we take in. Prana has all the colours of the elements.

As you progress in your practice along with the other exercises, the two channels of Ida and Pingala will clear of toxins and the central Sushumna channel will start functioning. This means that you are paving the way for the breath to move through the Sushumna.

Chapter Seven

The Breaths

The Eight Spiritual Breaths

1. The Memory Development Breath
2. The Revitalisation Breath
3. The Inspirational Breath
4. The Physical Perfection Breath
5. The Vibro-Magnetic Breath
6. The Cleansing Breath
7. The Grand Rejuvenation Breath
8. Your Own Spiritual Breath

You have to make a commitment to yourself that once you start the course, you will follow it till you complete it. Only a dedicated, determined practice delivers results and manifests the truths you are seeking and learning. If the practice is fragmented, the result will also be fragmented.

As you progress in the practice, you will be able to do each exercise for the required number of seven times. The time taken for doing the complete exercise can be anywhere between forty-five minutes to an hour. You will require an additional half-hour for meditation and its affirmation. The meditational affirmations are to be mentally recited slowly and with awareness.

With the prescribed Breathing Exercises that are being given here, you will be following the path of Descending Energy. With the first four Breaths, you will be cleansing all the chakras i.e. Sahasrar, Ajna, Vishuddhi, Anahat, Manipur, Swadhisthan and Muladhar chakras, with the emphasis on the first four.

It is only after having cleansed the chakras that you will move into the Breaths that will focus and activate the process of Ascending Energy.

When this method of Breathing Exercises and Affirmations is followed, the meridians and chakras will be cleared of any congestion and blocks related to emotional and psychological data that the individual body-mind organism might be carrying. The result will be a free and smooth flow of energy so that when the lower chakras are activated, and the powerful earth energy starts ascending, there are lesser chances of it getting trapped in any chakra.

As you practise daily, you will observe that when you breathe properly all the bodily functions work properly. The gross bulk of air that expands the lungs does not penetrate the muscles, nerve and bones. However, there is a subtle force within the air – the electric, vital fluid that is Prana – which goes everywhere.

The Affirmations have to be memorised and repeated as often as possible so that the thought penetrates to the subconscious mind to be absorbed and established. You may not see the sense of it now but it will unfold later; for now you are simply sending a message to the subconscious. It is like going back to school, where the child places total trust in what the teacher is teaching and in that trust the child grows up to reach the pinnacle of his career. You must have a child-like surrender to accept the teaching that is being given to you in the practise of the Breaths, and to follow the instructions. Keep an open mind; put aside all questions, doubts and fears. It is known that our lives are based on natural laws as definite in their operation as electricity, light, gravity and magnetism. Though these great laws are invisible to our eyes, we know they exist and what their effect is on things around us.

The Breaths and Affirmations that will follow are complete and aligned in a pattern in order to lead you into holistic awareness. They are to be practised strictly in the order they have been given. This point is being stressed because each

Breath will be creating a clear channel through which it flows. It is going to remove negative data that is blocking the free flow of Prana in the subtle body. If Prana is flowing freely in the meridians of the subtle body, then the flow of blood will also be smooth in the physical body. The Eight Breaths have been set in an order so that one smooth path is created for Prana to flow. By choosing a Breath at random, it means you are doing patchwork – leaving gaps in-between, and this will cause immense discomfort and disarray. You will lead the body-mind organism into a state of utter confusion.

The Vibro-Magnetic Breath is the midway point between the Breaths; from this Breath onwards the emphasis is more on the activating and awakening of the Manipur, Swadhisthan and Muladhar chakras. You must understand that while the Breaths may seem to be alike, they differ in their effect on the body-mind organism. Each is a different means of unlocking and balancing the energy. The work that is done in the physical organism when you are practising the Revitalisation Breath is quite different from that of the Memory Development Breath and so on. Be constantly aware of feelings that the Breaths generate. The Affirmations of each Breath have their own energy. They must be memorised and recited with awareness.

When you follow the sequence given by the Master, then the Creative Intelligence within you is giving it an appropriate direction so that it works towards manifesting your 'intention'. Understand that the breath is the vehicle of Prana. Once you surrender to the breath and allow it to take its own course during your practice, your sadhana will move smoothly. Do not use your mind to direct it, leave it to the spiritual force that dwells within you. It knows what is right for you; it will chart its own course. All the guidance that will come will be through the wisdom of your breath.

"We know that our lives are based on natural laws and though these are invisible, we know they exist, and they are powerful. No one saw gravity or electricity, but we know their effect. No one saw the force that pulls the compass needle towards the North Pole, but we know that it does pull it.

The Breaths

You never saw the force that makes you breathe, but you know that you do breathe. When we do the following Breaths, we go to the place where that force resides – in the Silence; and it is from the Silence that our knowledge will gradually break through from the great Universal storehouse."

– Swami K. S. Ramanathan

The Eight Breaths given along with their related Affirmations are to be done regularly, beginning with Pranayama. The Breathing Exercises should be performed comfortably and not in a rush. It is regular and consistent practise that will show results in due course. You need to be patient. Transformation cannot happen overnight. As you perfect your practice, you will see that each Breath is designed to interlock with the next, and they all have a distinct bearing on the physical body. Though these are physical breaths, they have an effect on the subtle bodies. As an aspirant you are urged to regard your body as a spiritual instrument, truly the temple of the living God, and to enter the practice with the deepest reverential frame of mind.

The Eight Breathing Exercises and Affirmations will bring balance to your mental, emotional and physical bodies. Please note that these Breathing Exercises have to be approached very gradually.

Except for the first Breath, The Memory Development Breath, which in the beginning has to be done seven times and gradually increased to forty nine times – for the other Breaths you have to start by doing each exercise two times and, gradually over weeks (as you get comfortable with them), do each Breath seven times. The Affirmation for each exercise has to follow the Breath before the start of the next exercise. Remember that the exercises have to be strictly done in sequence as they lock into each other. These Breathing Exercises are best if initially learned under the guidance of a teacher of Brahma Vidya. If, however, an aspirant is practising them on his own, he must stop if he feels any kind of discomfort. It could mean that he is not taking the breath in the required manner or that the posture is incorrect.

You can see that breath is your life. If we understand our breath, then we shall understand ourselves.

Chapter Eight

Affirmations

An affirmation is anything that we do or say. Anything that we keep thinking or repeating means that we are not just reciting but also affirming; thereby giving it power, and by doing that we create our experience. Invariably, what we say and think is life-negative; so, we continue to manifest life-negative experience. In order to change our experience from life-negative to life-positive, we have to learn to think in a positive manner. Instead of the mind directing us, we need to learn to direct the mind. It is like having a hold on the reins of the horse you are riding. You consciously manoeuvre it in the direction you want it to go. In the same manner, you have to have a conscious control of your mind. This requires a great deal of practise. It means that we consciously choose words that will either help eliminate something unwanted from our life, or help create something new in our life.

Some of our thoughts and superstitions belong to the collective thought patterns or affirmations of our belief system. These we start imbibing from our childhood, only to realise at some stage how our beliefs are limiting us. Maybe they were appropriate in the times of our grandparents or their parents, but no longer serve any purpose today. It is like my grandmother telling me that if I cut my nails at night, it would be unlucky. She refused to understand that we now have electricity and there was no fear of cutting my finger instead of the nail. We need to weed out what is no longer relevant to our growth. If we constantly express or affirm lack in our life, be it lack of wealth or relationships or lack of anything, then lack is what we are going to manifest.

Affirmations

We are at a stage where our consciousness has expanded and an understanding has come that our thoughts create our experience, and therefore our lives. Things will not change overnight. A great deal of positive data has to be fed into the mind so that the negative data starts surfacing and moving out. Each morning, before moving into the day, we can express our gratitude and consciously choose positive thoughts or affirmations that we have created for ourselves to have a happy and productive day.

"Affirmative statements are 'going beyond the reality of the present into the creation of the future through the words you use in the now'. If you say 'I want to... or I have to'... you are always in the future. It has to be 'I have...' As you change your thinking process, then everything in your life will change. Such is the power of thought."

– Neale Donald Walsch

"Your thoughts are pure vibration; they can and do create your experience."

– Louise L. Hay

You are an aspirant who is seeking answers. The Breathing Exercises and their Affirmations are designed to give you those answers. Some of you who get into the practice may move quickly, while others may take time. A serious and dedicated aspirant is sure to get results as he progresses on the journey. All Affirmations are to be emotionally charged and recited with appropriate feeling. Swami Ramanathan tells us: "In your day-to-day living, you first think, then you feel, and then you act." So, the pattern we follow is: thinking, feeling and putting into action the thought. The most important factor is 'feeling'. All Affirmations are to be recited with feeling; mere intellectual repetition will not give results. Because you feel, you know that whatever you are affirming will manifest. This conviction must, therefore, be firmly established in your mind. Also, this conviction must pass from the mental sphere into the feeling, so that not only do you feel that you know it to be a certainty, but you know that you feel it to be a certainty. Do you see the difference? You must know that you feel it.

After completing the required number of cycles for Pranayama, and the Breathing Exercises along with their Affirmations, it is important that you sit quietly for ten minutes watching the inhalation and exhalation of your breath.

Louise L. Hay , author of *You Can Heal Your Life*, explains that your beliefs are merely habitual thinking patterns that you learned as a child. Some of these beliefs may limit your ability to create the very things you want. You need to pay attention to your thoughts so that you can eliminate the ones creating experiences that you don't want. Affirmations mean – consciously choosing words that will either help eliminate something from your life or help create something in your life.

Chapter Nine

1. The Memory Development Breath

As you now begin to practise the first Breath, it must be stressed that care should be taken to start slowly and not rush into the practice in the enthusiasm to get quick results. If you do that, you can exhaust your lungs, heart and other organs of the body along with your nervous system, thus causing damage. There should be no violent respirations, no extended holding of breath beyond a comfortable measure. What is required is patience and perseverance. Even though initially you may not find a difference, you are progressing all the time at the gross level as well as the subtle level.

The basic requirement is an upright, comfortable position during practice so that the flow of breath is not disturbed. After the first month, you will be eagerly looking forward to the new knowledge that gradually starts coming to you while you sit in meditation. If you are a true seeker, perhaps before you even become aware of the effect your practice is creating, you will realise that the course follows the dictum:

> *"Ask and it will be given to you; seek and you will find; knock and the door will be opened to you. For everyone who asks receives; he who seeks finds; and to him who knocks, the door will be opened."*
>
> – Matthew 7:7

This Breath cleanses and takes from our memory that which is negative and weak, bringing the memory to a state of clarity and purity.

The Eight Spiritual Breaths

Posture for the Memory Development Breath

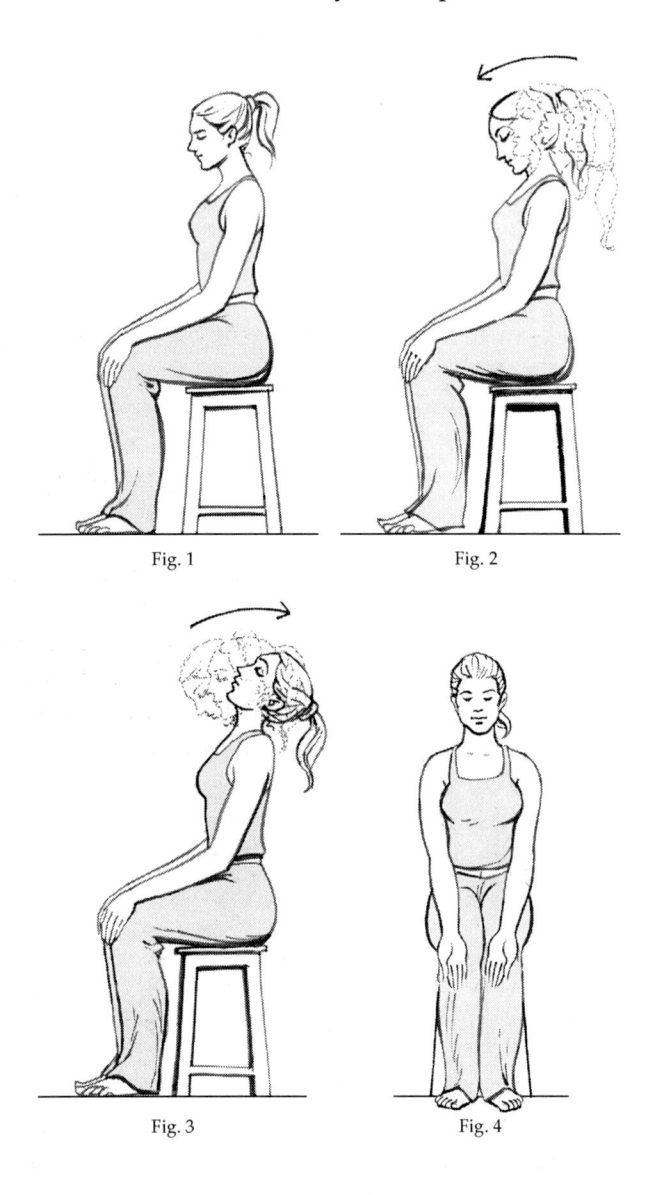

Fig. 1

Fig. 2

Fig. 3

Fig. 4

Note: This Breathing Exercise is powerful. Please follow the instructions carefully.

The Memory Development Breath

Practising the Memory Development Breath

Sit in a straight-backed chair or stool, with the spine erect. Hands on the thighs, palms downward. Heels must be together with the toes slightly apart. Shoulders relaxed (not drawn up), with no tension in the neck.

In this position, start the rhythmic action by moving the head backward without strain, and without moving the rest of the body: then moving it forward and downward till the chin touches the base of the throat.

1. As the head swings back, take a deep breath in through the nostrils (evenly and smoothly).

2. As soon as the inhalation is complete with the backward swing of the head, start exhaling vigorously through the teeth while the head swings forward and downward with the sound 'shhhhhhh' – a deep forceful exhalation.

3. Repeat this process of inhalation through the nostrils (as the head swings back) and exhalation through the teeth vigorously and forcefully (as the head swings forward and downward), seven times (seven swings back, and seven swings forward) without pause: the forward motion of the head beginning as soon as the backward motion stops.

Rest a few moments, watching and feeling the different sensations in your body. Then do another seven breaths and rest for a few moments. Do this until seven sevens have been breathed, i.e. forty-nine times. Backward and forward is one cycle. As you become familiar with this exercise, you may do seven breaths and after a few moments rest, do three rounds of fourteen breaths each, taking a few moments of rest after each round.

Be alert that you do not lean back in the chair or slouch. The spine has to be kept straight. This is a rhythmic breath: the head gently swings backward and forward, without a jerk, like a pendulum. The swing backward should be slow and smooth in order to allow complete inhalation; then, immediately begin the forward swing of the head with simultaneous exhalation, timed in order that the complete breath is exhaled as it reaches the lowest point. Remember that the breath is to be taken through the nostrils as the head swings back, and is breathed out through the mouth when the head swings forward and down. The head tilting fully back and then fully forward is one cycle. For the first week you can do it only seven times; for the next week you can add fourteen more to it; that will make it twenty-one, followed by the Affirmation. You go on adding till you reach forty-nine swings. At the final count, inhale and relax, place your hands on the knees palms facing up and mentally repeat the Affirmation for this Breath, as given here.

When over a period of time you have mastered the rhythmic pendulum-like movement of this Breath, then you can do the exercise at a stretch from count one to forty-nine.

The Memory Development Breath

Affirmation and Visualisation

I see a bright light over my head.

To be memorised:

"I now see a bright light above my head. The top of my head feels heavy yet relaxed, my forehead is relaxed, my eyes feel heavy and relaxed, the muscles of my face are relaxed, my teeth rest lightly on each other, my jaw eases gently, my arms and hands feel very heavy... Yet, I feel so happy. I feel so completely happy, my beautiful face is happy and smiling. My entire body is aglow with the flush of my smiles. There is a light pressure building inside me and moving outwards, removing all my cares, worries, troubles and fears... I feel happy in every pore of my being.

"The light now comes down. My chest feels lighter; my abdomen is relaxed as the light travels right down to the tips of my toes.

"I now imagine that strong light behind my neck. I see myself looking all the way down my beautiful spine. I feel I'm looking at a *great waterfall, with the sunlight playing on it. I see countless specks of sparkling light... and I know my whole body is full of light, light, light.*

"If your eye be single," the Single Eye, the Eternal Eye, the Third Eye, the Spiritual Eye, the Eye that I am now using...

"If your eye be single, your whole body will be full of light.

"I know that each cell in the countless number of cells in my body is a light, a lamp, a torch, bringing the light of the Divine wisdom within me – the light being in perfect harmony with the flame, as the flame is in perfect harmony with the fire... the fire of Divine love that is in the innermost centre of my being.

"Now, feeling happy and giving thanks...without letting myself know it, I take a little breath and then a long drawn-out, deep sigh.

"Again, I take another little breath... and a quick sigh."

Effect of the Breathing Exercise and Affirmation

You will see that total faith and regularity in your practice will give you greater energy of body, power of thought, alertness, enthusiasm, drive and more strength of character.

The Memory Development Breath, which is the first Breath you will be practising, is a wonder breath. Glands in the neck and throat are exercised. The muscles and the bones at the back of the neck are lubricated. This Breath alone will bring untold benefits to you.

Cleansing and activating the chakras

With this Breath, you are accessing grace. This means you are going to follow the path of Descending Energy i.e. you will start working from the Sahasrar centre downwards to the Ajna, Vishuddhi, Anahata, Manipur, Swadhisthan and Muladhar chakras. This is different from the alternate path where work begins with the lowest chakra, Muladhar, and the energy works its way upwards.

While cleansing all the chakras, this Breath enhances the activity of Sahasrar, Ajna and Vishuddhi chakras.

Vibrations of the Sahasrar centre

At times when this centre is in motion, the speed of its rotation deflects vibrations that send out sparks that look like petals.

Sahasrar: Beyond the body, the Sahasrar is associated with Cosmic Consciousness. Its colour is luminous white and silver. The sole purpose of this centre in the subtle body is to connect the individual consciousness with infinite energies; to utilise those energies to its advantage; to know the unknown; to tune in and surrender to the Cosmic Consciousness; to experience the transcendental meaning of life, oneness and bliss. Sahasrar is the abode of the individual's higher consciousness. When this centre opens and expands, the individual transcends mundane or individual awareness of the 'I', 'you' and 'they'. One rises above name and form.

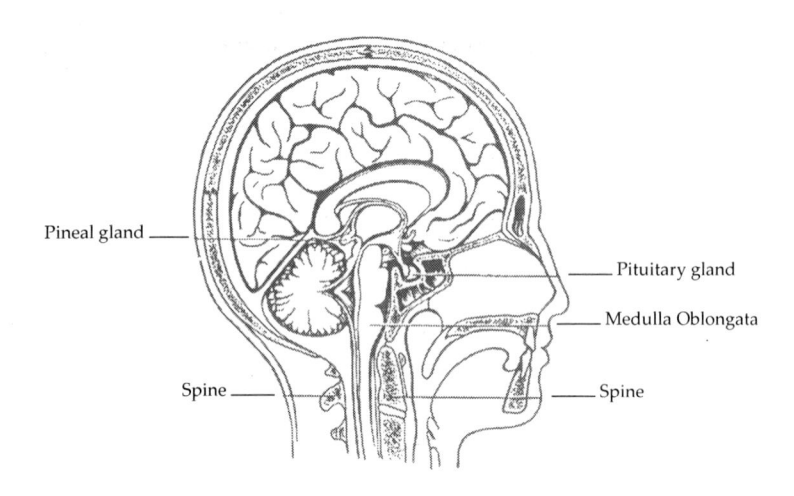

The pineal gland is also called the Third eye. It connects the physical and spiritual world. The pineal gland is about the size of a pea and is in the centre of the brain in a tiny cave behind and above the pituitary gland, which lies a little behind the roof of the nose.

Vibrations of the Ajna chakra

These vibrations, resembling wings, emanate from the centre of the brow and side of the temples when the chakra is active.

Ajna chakra: This chakra is the point where the three main nadis – Ida, Pingala and Sushumna, merge into one stream of consciousness and flow up to Sahasrar, the Crown Centre. Ajna means 'command', 'perception', 'knowledge' and 'authority'. In the body it is associated with the pineal gland, eyes and brain. Its Tattva is *Maha Tattva*, in which all other Tattvas are present in their rarefied, pure essence. Its colour is purple and indigo. The development of this chakra helps an individual to move from dualistic mind to intuitive neutral mind. This means one moves away from opposites and accepts things as they are without judging them. Working with Ajna helps to focus the mind, bringing forth clarity, peace, inner and cosmic knowledge. Ajna is the bridge that links the guru with the disciples. It represents the level at which it is possible for direct mind-to-mind communication between two people.

Ajna is referred to as the Third eye, the Divine eye, or the eye of intuition that gazes inwards and outwards, thus developing the power of insight and foresight. In the practise of the Breathing Exercises, it acts as the control centre for the distribution of Prana. If the vision of light at the Ajna is well developed, an aspirant is able to visualise the flow and movement of Prana.

Vibrations of the Vishuddhi chakra

The purplish-blue vibrations of the expanded Vishuddhi chakra.

Vishuddhi chakra: The name means 'pure'. In the body, it is associated with the throat, ears, thyroid, parathyroid, and with the element 'ether'. The element (Tattva) of the Vishuddhi chakra is Cosmos (sound) and the sense organ is the ear. Its colour is a combination of pale purple and royal blue. The development of this chakra gives the gift of expressing one's truth (experience) without fear, and to transmit and receive knowledge of the Truth. It creates a vibrational relationship with all existence. With the development of this chakra the mind becomes pure, and the purifying and harmonising of all opposites takes place. The developed Vishuddhi represents a state of openness in which life is viewed as the provider of all experiences that lead to greater understanding. One no longer continues to avoid unpleasant aspects of life and seek only the pleasant. Instead, there is an acceptance of allowing things to happen in a way that they are ordained to happen. Proper understanding and true discrimination comes out of this equal acceptance of the opposites or dualities of life. One is also helped to differentiate between realisation coming into one's consciousness from higher realms and the mere chatter of unconscious and wishful thinking. An aspirant, whose Vishuddhi chakra is active, develops the ability of neutralising the effect of the negative

The Memory Development Breath

aspects that come up in his life and so enables him to dissolve any problems that would otherwise manifest as physical symptoms.

The vibrations in this chakra are usually felt as a fluttering of wings in the throat; the impression is that of a small bird or a butterfly. In the visual on the facing page, the Vishuddhi chakra is active and its range of vibration can expand according to the need of the moment.

If the Breath is performed correctly, those who get the vision to see the subtle form may sense or feel how negative data is thrown out.

The purpose of this Breath is to charge the body with Prana, the subtle force of life, nerve and brain energy, to start you on the road of higher consciousness. One of the essentials of this higher consciousness is the feeling of joy and beauty, and of light and Divine love within.

Chapter Ten

2. The Revitalisation Breath

We know that with right breathing our physical health improves. The same beneficial effect is experienced by the mind; we are happier and in a positive state of mind. Spiritually we are at peace. This is because with correct breathing we bring in more light into the body, mind and spirit, and we see things and situations in the right perspective.

Having thoroughly cleansed and energised every cell in the brain with the Memory Development Breath, we need to revitalise the physical body. The Revitalisation Breath helps to distribute the energy – cleansing, breaking down the physical and mental blocks, resulting in the circulation and free flow of energy that we bring down with the Breath.

You will find that time and again during the course of practice, emphasis is laid on correct breathing so that the body-mind organism is purified and becomes sensitive to the universal force flowing in with each breath. It is only when you feel it that you will know it. The Revitalisation Breath starts this process.

When you perform this Breath, feel the Prana rushing into you. Imagine it coming into you as light, revitalising every cell in your body.

The Eight Spiritual Breaths

Posture for the Revitalisation Breath

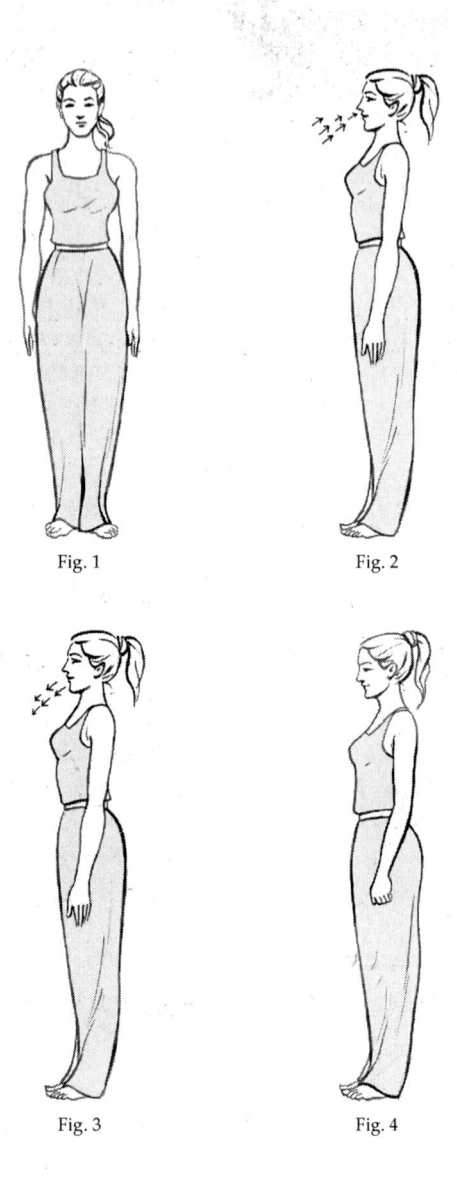

Fig. 1

Fig. 2

Fig. 3

Fig. 4

Note: This Breathing Exercise is powerful. Please follow the instructions carefully.

The Revitalisation Breath

Visualisation of the Breath

As you breathe in, visualise your chest expanding and filling with light as the breath goes right down to the Muladhar chakra. The exhaled breath throws out all impurities, leaving the passage full of light.

Practising the Revitalisation Breath

Commence with two breaths; gradually increase to seven breaths over one or two weeks. All breaths from now onwards are done in a standing posture.

Stand erect and see that the spine is straight, heels together, toes apart, stomach in and buttocks tight.

1. First, breathe through the nostrils inhaling steadily but not too slowly. Commence breathing deep down in the abdomen, filling the lower part of the lungs, then the middle part, then the upper part. You will find that if you inhale properly the abdomen will be drawn in slightly.

2. Retain the breath for about thirty seconds.

3. Now exhale vigorously through the puckered lips with the 'shhhhhhh' sound. The chest must not be relaxed – hold it firm. As the breath escapes, draw in the abdomen tightly and lift it upwards. Let out every bit of air, pressing the abdomen in.

4. Then inhale and relax the chest and the whole body, breathing in and out as rhythmically as possible, mentally repeating the spiritual Affirmation for this Breath as given on the following page.

Affirmation and Visualisation

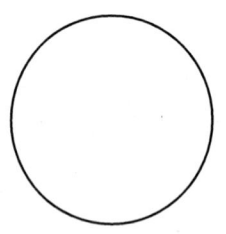

Visualising a circle, symbolising 'wholeness', say the Affirmation given below audibly.

In order to get the right result, the Affirmation should be recited consciously with full vigour and enthusiasm and not in a lazy and lax manner.

Now we relax entirely – coming right down – relaxing – relaxing entirely – as we think of the inner, hidden meaning of these sublimely simple words:

To be memorised:

The Nine Positives:

"I am whole... perfectly whole. Nothing is missing – nothing to be added... I am whole!

"I am perfect.

"I am strong.

"I am powerful, all-powerful. Each cell in my body is a power plant working for me. I am powerful.

"I am loving.

"I am harmonious – I'm in harmony with the Laws – the External, Enduring, Unchanging, Everlasting Laws of the universe.

"I am rich.

"I am young. And now that liquid feeling in the body, as if many streams of liquid light are rushing downwards in my body.

"I am happy. I feel happy, I look happy, I am happy.

"Giving thanks and feeling happy, I now take a little breath and a long deep sigh. I take another little breath, and a quick sigh."

The Revitalisation Breath

After the vigorous Memory Development Breath where the Sahasrar, Ajna and Vishuddhi chakras were thoroughly energised and the toxins thrown out, you have the Revitalisation Breath. This is a deep breath going right down from the Ajna chakra to the Muladhar chakra. Its gentle inhalation and vigorous exhalation helps further in throwing out the toxins. In due course, this Breath will now align the energised and active chakras and bring them into balance. The qualities of these chakras will be further enhanced.

Ajna, along with its attributes, will further unfold psychic receptivity through which the guidance of the guru and the higher self is initiated. Vishuddhi chakra will bestow insight and discrimination. Anahat chakra, our emotional heart, when fully awakened will bestow universal love and compassion. The Manipur chakra that controls the digestive system and is the major distributor of energy, when awakened, will enhance the qualities of charisma and heroism. *Swadhisthan* chakra is the threshold of the unconscious mind and will bring up the stored data of desires, inhibitions, talents, intuition, demons and deities. Muladhar chakra is the seat of the primal energy, the source of both our sensuality and spirituality. It represents the instinctive mind.

The knowledge that is being imparted to you has to be clearly understood. Just as a seed is sown in fertile soil and has to be tended in order to grow, similarly the seed of spiritual knowledge when sowed, needs proper nourishment and this is provided by the Breathing Exercises, meditation and selfless service. With correct breathing, we bring in with the breath that rhythmic, universal force that corresponds to the elements that create the body. The more rhythmically we breathe, the more we feel Prana as a force.

The words of the spiritual Affirmations are the seeds that you are sowing. They will grow within you, developing the conditions contemplated and expressed, exactly in proportion to the feelings with which you recite them. You must begin to develop the power of imagination and visualisation, the creative faculties with which we all work. This means you must create pictures in your mind of those conditions that you wish to realise. Thought is an immeasurable force and you are using it for all purposes, every moment of your life. I have seen my thoughts as I went through the course, and whatever I was affirming, I would see its form. I would see not only the form, but also all the subtleties involved in that thought which at the conscious level I would not know. One thought form triggers a sequence of thought forms. So, rest assured that all thoughts have forms and the potential to actualise. As you go along with your practice, you may also be on your way to developing this faculty of sensing or seeing thought forms.

In 'The Nine Positives' are the qualities that the Revitalisation Breath endeavours to instil in you so that you can manifest them into your mundane life. Do not doubt, do not fear, and have a childlike surrender.

"I am Whole." In a relaxed state of mind, think of the word 'Whole'. A sensation of roundness will probably come into your mind. Now, think outwards from the mind and you will sense the expanding roundness. Feel this sensation of roundness and wholeness. Lose yourself in it so that in the expansion, as thought ceases, you experience yourself in the expanded state as that blissful wholeness.

Because of body-consciousness, fragmented personality, compulsive thinking and exteriorisation of mind, the experience of being 'Whole' is lost. When you reach the stage in your daily living where you can touch the awareness inside, the Divine force given by the God within, irrespective of the religion and creed, you will experience the sense of Wholeness.

Wholeness is within you. If you project your thought through that wholeness, it is bound to fructify! When you are apprehensive of doing anything, watch your approach, or how you act, how you speak and notice the level of your confidence – *atma-vishvas*. The way you talk makes the difference. A successful man talks in a way which can convince other people. An unsuccessful person may have better knowledge, but he is not capable of putting it into practise. Atma-vishvas is very important and the best way to define atma-vishvas is 'I am Whole'. When you are Whole, the whole universe, of which you are a part, is Whole. Where is the question of any fear or apprehension? Where is the question of things not happening? 'I am Whole'. This is further explained as, "Nothing is lacking in you and nothing can be added to you." If anything is whole, the question of anything lacking does not arise.

An example would be a bucket full of water. You can add nothing more to it because it is already full. Similarly, if you are Whole, nothing can be added, because you are Whole.

Now when you say this Affirmation, you have to say it with a strong feeling for it to be effective. Over a period of time, when you go on repeating it and it enters your subconscious mind, it will make all the difference, even to your physical appearance, your walk, your speech and eventually your performance.

"**I am Perfect.**" When you think of the word 'Perfect', the sensation in the mind is different from that when you think of the word 'Whole'. Meditate on the two words and notice the difference in the feelings of the two words. Register the feeling so that you can bring it back when you desire to do so. If you are 'Whole', you are bound to be 'Perfect'. Imperfection comes when something is lacking in you. But, if you are Whole, you are bound to be Perfect. 'Whole' in Sanskrit is called *Poorna*. I am Whole – I am Poorna, I am Perfect – I am *Paripoorna*.

So, you are Perfect. As a representative of God, you become responsible for whatever work you undertake to do; to see that it is done with honesty and integrity. Always look at nature. It is perfect in every respect: in the movements of the solar system, in your body functions, in flora and fauna. Nature does its work without any discrimination.

"**I am Strong.**" When you think of the word 'Strong', register the sensation that arises in your mind and extend it to your body. This is important because it will be in accordance with the idea of strength that you identify with – as in the case of imagining an elephant. See which symbol arises in your mind when you think of the word 'Strong'. What came up for me was the wind.

Now, if you are 'Whole' and you are 'Perfect', you are bound to be 'Strong'. Here we must understand the difference between 'Strong' and 'Powerful'.

'Strong'. Create a picture of strength, like *Hanuman*, an elephant, etc. Strength is that which is given under certain circumstances and at certain times when one uses one's maximum strength to the fullest. When I am lifting a weight of 200 lbs., that is my strength. It is the optimum I can do in a given set of circumstances. 'I am Strong'. When you say this repeatedly over a period of time, you will find a tremendous strength developing within you – when you walk, when you work, when you exercise. The moment you say that you feel weak – your metabolism starts changing immediately. So, always affirm: "I am Strong."

"**I am Powerful.**" This is also to be expressed as above. Feel what 'Power' means to you and then see what symbol comes up. For me, it was the ocean.

Every cell in my body is like a power plant working for me. I am Powerful. What is Power? Power is that for whatever you do, you have the power supply to the extent you need it. Otherwise you feel tired, exhausted, frustrated. That is why you should say, "I am Powerful." The body has six trillion cells working for you with three trillion reactions per second and when you allow the potential of these cells to work for you, you are at your best.

Now these Recitations – I am Whole, I am Perfect, I am Strong, I am Powerful – are connected to the Infinite Potential within you. You have trillions of cells. Every cell has DNA; though microscopic, its information and knowledge would fill thousands of volumes because it is connected to Totality's wisdom. Such is the infinity inside each cell.

Create an example of anything you consider powerful.

"I am Loving." Think of love, of its changeless nature, of its essence, in whatever form it may be presented to your mind. There are different aspects to love. See whether you can comprehend what the 'Love of God' truly means. To me, it is expressed through nature. Love that we understand in ordinary parlance is from the preconceived notions that we have developed from the time we were born till this moment. The love of parents, siblings and friends is one kind of love. Love is also connected to sex. Unfortunately, from the influence of the books we read and the movies we see, it is popularly perceived that it is impossible for men and women to have a loving relationship without a sexual aspect. However, sexual love is only one aspect of love. While love is connected to sex, love can go beyond sex.

We must learn to understand what real love is. Love is so great that if the question is asked how God can be felt in mundane life, the answer will be, through love. And how can we experience the presence of God? Only through love.

Be receptive to God. Ask Him to transmit to you the feeling, the pouring of emotion. Ask God to let you be aware of and to feel love.

"I am Harmonious." Think of harmony, rhythm, equilibrium and the poise of the universe. Think of the order of the universe. These thoughts should filter from the mind into the feeling, and the feeling should be so deeply registered that you can avail of it any time. If you are Whole, you are Perfect, you are Strong, you are Powerful, you are Loving; then naturally, you will be Harmonious. There is a concept in Hinduism that says that ultimately God wanted to enjoy Himself, Consciousness wanted to enjoy Itself, and therefore, He created the universe as His *leela* or play. From that point of view, the embodiments are created in this world in such a way that there will be harmony and blissful conditions in the universe. Look to nature, there is nothing more harmonious than nature in all its forms.

"I am Rich." Think of the unfailing supply of the universe. You are rich. Nothing is lacking. Think of nature, which is ever providing in abundance.

"I am Young." Imagine that your body is in a liquid state from head to toe. Imagine innumerable streams of light flowing downwards; see them clearly flowing down.

"I am Happy." Imagine that you are looking upwards over the top of your head. Now, send your thought of happiness up through your head. Then, relax the mind and the body and imagine that every cell in the body is being charged with joy, which is the vital fluid that propels the forces of the very universe.

In this exercise, you are bringing all the forces of your body into perfect rhythm. You are bringing them all into one direction, just as in the light of an electric bulb all the molecules are magnetised to flow in one direction.

Chapter Eleven

3. The Inspirational Breath

Thousands of years ago, the great sages developed a powerful system of breath control. They used this for mastering fear, for healing, and for attaining enlightenment. The science of these Breaths possesses remarkable powers, for they tap into the Breath of Life – the spiritual life force that gives our breath its life-sustaining power. Our breath is the vehicle for Prana – the life force.

Because our breath is so intimately linked with the life force or Prana, it controls every mental, emotional and physical process that takes place in our being. Every experience of pain and fear is controlled by this Breath. It also contains some of the most powerful healing energies, the mastering of which can enable us to heal ourselves in body, mind and spirit. Spiritual Masters have said, "Always practise awareness of your breath, for when that is maintained it brings many benefits and blessings. All that you are doing is to find out what life is, what the origin of life is, and what the continuation of life is – what it is that causes it all."

The Eight Spiritual Breaths

Posture for the Inspirational Breath

Fig. 1

Fig. 2

Fig. 3

Fig. 4

Fig. 5

Note: This Breathing Exercise is powerful. Please follow the instructions carefully.

The Inspirational Breath

Practising the Inspirational Breath

Keep in mind that these exercises are to be done in the sequence they are given along with their Affirmations.

If the mind wanders while you are doing the exercises, you might mix up the sequence and do the third exercise as the second and the second exercise as the third. Care has to be taken that you do not mix up the sequence because then you will be confusing the energy that is flowing down. If you have missed one exercise, it is better to let it pass and move on to the next in sequence.

Commence with two breaths; gradually increase to seven breaths over one or two weeks.

Stand erect and see that the spine is straight, heels together, toes apart, stomach in and buttocks tight.

1. Inhale a complete breath. Be rigid. Buttocks tight. Feet firm on the ground. Raise the rigid arms slowly until the hands touch above the head, palms outwards with the thumbs crossed and the forefinger tips touching. See that you are rigid, and that you are reaching as high as possible, but without any disturbance in your feet (no tip-toeing), the backs of your hands touching.

2. Retain the breath for two to three seconds, not more.

3. Now lower the hands to forty-five degrees from the shoulders, exhaling a little air vigorously through your puckered lips. Then lower your arms, level with your shoulders, and exhale vigorously a little more. Then lower them again a little, and let out more breath but with the chest as firm as a rock all the time. Then lower them to the sides and thoroughly empty the lungs, pulling the abdomen in, exhaling vigorously through puckered lips with the 'shhhhhhh' sound. Remember, buttocks stay firm. At the final count, inhale and relax, mentally repeating the spiritual Affirmation for this Breath as given on the following page.

Affirmation and Visualisation

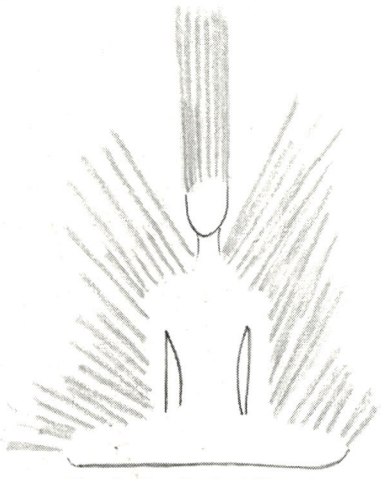

Visualisation for the Affirmation.

To be memorised:

Always maintain an attitude of gratitude. Stand with folded hands and consciously recite the Affirmation. Your body is the instrument – it is the temple of the living God. If the instrument is not perfect, how can receptivity be perfect?

Now, we relax entirely... coming right down... relaxing the whole body.

"I thank you Lord, for my body. I thank you Law – Eternal, Unchangeable Law of my being – for my body that is the most beautiful, intricate, and most precise instrument in this universe.

"My body, which is the temple of the Living God, the temple of the God who lives within me, is alive within me.

"I thank you Lord for my body.

"I revere the wisdom stored in the very substance of my body, and I vow that from this moment henceforth, nothing that I shall do or say or think, eat and drink, shall abuse this temple of the Living God, my body.

"And now, feeling happy, giving thanks, I take a little breath and a long, deep, sweeping, sweeping sigh... and now I take another little breath, and a quick sigh."

Effect of the Breathing Exercise and Affirmation

Breath is the fountain of all human power. Today, television can project sound and picture around the earth in seconds. What is this transporting force? It is ether and it is everywhere in the atmosphere. We also take in this same powerful ether in the air with our breath. You should become conscious of it and utilise its vast resources to your benefit. Your physical health depends on correct breathing. Your mental health, happiness, self-control, clear-sightedness and morale also depend very largely on the way you breathe.

All the Breathing Exercises constantly work to cleanse the chakras. After energising and activating the Sahasrar, Ajna and Vishuddhi chakras, you now get down to work on expanding the Anahat chakra. You will notice that the process is very gradual so as not to send the chakras into a panic but to tune them to work in synchronicity.

Visualisation of the Anahat chakra

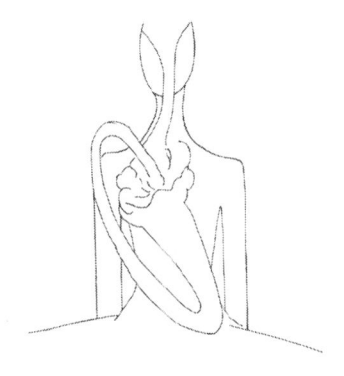

This visual shows the constant functioning of the Creative Intelligence within us.

Anahat chakra: With this Breathing Exercise, the Anahat chakra flowers fully. The Ajna chakra extends itself. Moving through the Vishuddhi chakra, down to the Manipur chakra, it takes a U-turn and enters the flowering Anahat chakra. All knowledge gathered at different centres is assimilated in the Heart chakra. Realisation of self-worth, self-love, compassion and the healing ability through touch or radiating energy are the attributes of a developed Anahat chakra.

Its element is air (touch) and its sense organ is the skin. Sensation is felt in the body from the aspect of the Anahat chakra relating to the person inside the body. Hugging, therefore, is a heart chakra activity. When one hugs, one is aware of what the person inside the other body feels, and he/she is aware of what you feel inside your body – there is a sense of relating to the person inside the body.

The Inspirational Breath

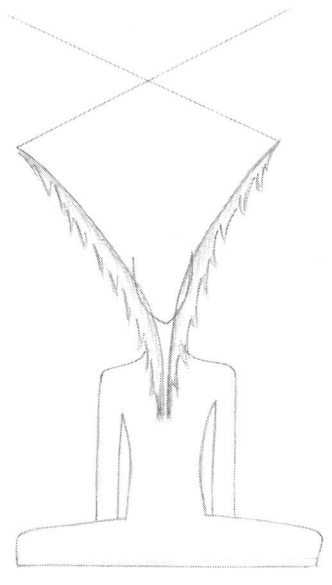

The vibrations of Anahat chakra give the feeling of having 'wings' and as they move to a higher vibratory level they cross each other, synchronising the emotional and mental bodies, thus bringing them into balance.

Vibrations of Anahat chakra.

In the physical body, the Anahat chakra relates to the thymus gland that is located in the upper anterior portion of the chest cavity just behind the sternum.

Chapter Twelve

4. The Physical Perfection Breath

The Physical Perfection Breath is the fourth Breath. In the previous three Breaths, you have cleansed and coordinated the whole body. Every muscle is developed, every nerve is charged and purified – every cell has been awakened and charged with energy, and the realisation dawns that our body is the 'most beautiful, intricate and precise instrument in this universe'.

The Universal Force that we bring in with the breath is locked up within us. It is only when the body starts transcending from the gross to the subtle level of vibration achieved through the dedicated practise of the Breaths, that this life force within can be sensed and felt. You are working towards achieving perfection in body and in mind, so you can tune in to your true nature.

The Eight Spiritual Breaths

Posture for the Physical Perfection Breath

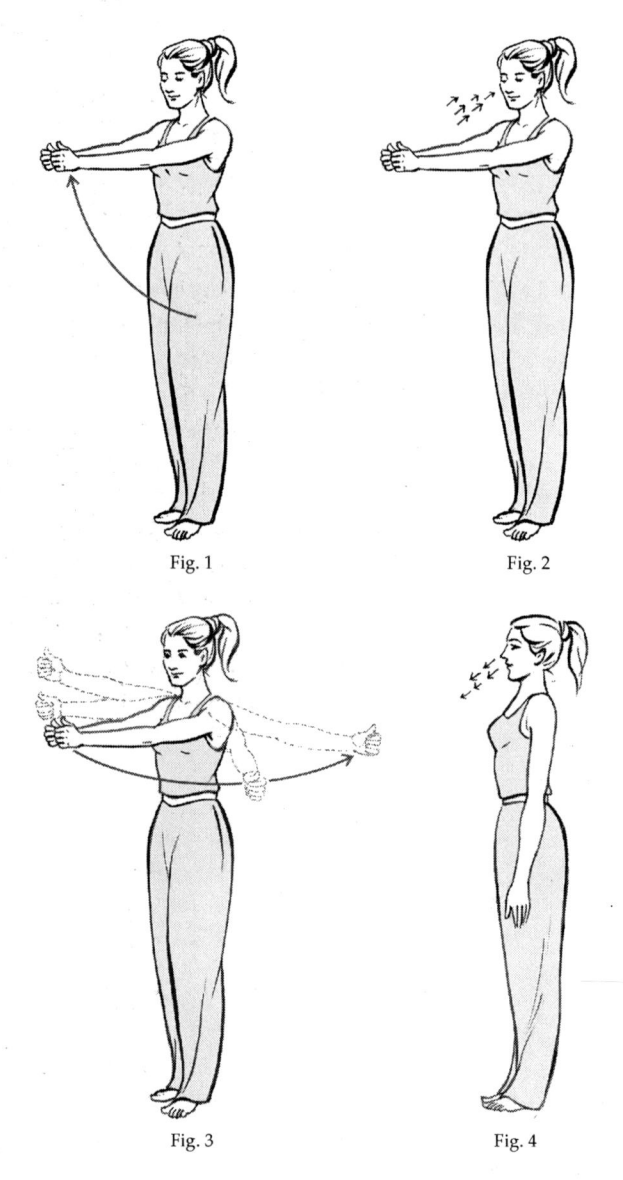

Fig. 1

Fig. 2

Fig. 3

Fig. 4

Note: This Breathing Exercise is powerful. Please follow the instructions carefully.

The Physical Perfection Breath

Practising the Physical Perfection Breath

Commence with two breaths; gradually increase to seven breaths over one or two weeks.

Stand erect and see that the spine is straight, heels together, toes apart, stomach in and buttocks tight.

1. Extend your arms straight in front of you, with palms of the hands together (or with fists clenched) and the arms comfortably firm but not too rigid. See that you are standing firmly on your feet with the sense that you are gripping the floor. Have your body perfectly straight and firm.

2. Inhale a complete breath. Retain your breath.

3. Standing very firmly, buttocks tight, swing the arms back as far as they will go without bending them, so that you 'stretch' the chest, as you swing the arms back. Bring them to the front again, seeing that you allow no breath to escape. Do this three times. Then bring the arms to your sides, exhale 'shhhhhhh' vigorously (through the mouth) as in the earlier exercises.

After the seventh count inhale and relax, mentally repeating the spiritual Affirmation for this Breath as given on the following page.

The Eight Spiritual Breaths

Affirmation and Visualisation

To the right of the chest lies the spiritual heart where the Creator dwells.

To be memorised:

And now relaxing entirely, relaxing the whole body, we prepare ourselves to think of the greatest thought we ever shall be able to think:

"Whatever the Creator is, I am.

"The Creator is right here... here in the heart of me... in the substance of me... in the mind of me... right in the being of me.

"Reveal yourself, O, Lord of my Life. Come, I wait... I listen... I look within... I am still. Now, I will to see the Creator at work within the temple of my body and giving thanks, feeling happy, ever so softly, without letting myself know it, I take a little breath and a long, deep sigh.

"I now take another little breath and a quick sigh."

The Physical Perfection Breath

Effect of the Breathing Exercise and Affirmation

This Breath helps to further expand the Anahat chakra with the result that you develop the freedom to determine your destiny. Once the Heart chakra is open and fully developed, then what you think or wish comes to pass. This puts a great responsibility on what you think and say. All negative thoughts are to be shunned.

There is great depth to the Affirmations and you need to contemplate on them. You are working to attain perfection in body and mind so that you may realise your true nature.

The creative force is omniscient, omnipresent and omnipotent. This force is the origin of all things and there is not a single embodiment of life where it is not in existence. How you receive the knowledge that is being revealed to you depends on your intuition and power of thought. We now come to the understanding that the universe and God are not separate; that the created and the Creator are one. God is in man and man is in God.

You are now laying the foundation. Therefore, be humble of mind like a child and true knowledge will come to you faster. The Truth is very simple, it is in our constant questioning and debating that it keeps slipping from us. You are advised to drop all that you have learned so far and which you have not tested in the acid test of your own experience. There should be no conflict in your thinking. Just follow what you are being guided to do and everything will unfold gradually.

It is one thing to read about the Truth but it is quite another to experience it. If you don't experience it, you will not know it. It will not become a part of you. Mere knowledge of it will not do anything for you.

The Affirmations are designed and empowered to lead you to the truth of who you are by consciously directing and manoeuvring your mind in the direction you want it to go. It is like having a hold on the reins of the horse you are riding. In the same manner, you must have a conscious control of your mind. This requires a great deal of practise. It means that we consciously choose words that will either help eliminate something unwanted from our life, or help create something new in our life. Affirmations are the key to the results you are seeking. You have to be diligent in your practice. I can only show you the 'how' of what I did. The doing was mine. I followed the instructions and believed whatever I was told. There were no doubts or questions, just a complete conscious surrender to the teaching.

Chapter Thirteen

5. The Vibro-Magnetic Breath

It sometimes happens that when you are into the practise of the Breaths, your mind has wandered and you have lost count of the number of times you have done the exercise, or there is no coherence in the recitation of the Affirmation. This means that the breath is ruled by the mind. As you progress in your practice, you will become aware of the fickle functioning of the mind. Once this awareness arises, it is the breath that rules the mind and can direct it in the appropriate direction, thus leading it to give the desired result. It is only when the breath is cool and calm and the mind peaceful, that one can look within. It is in that relaxed state of mind that certain centres of the brain open up and release the ancient data stored, sometimes relating to earlier lifetimes. There is no computer yet to match the human brain and its capacity to store up lifetimes of data. We are privileged to be able to replace the old data with new, and discharge what is no longer relevant and required. Lifetimes of stored conditioning can be discarded and what is relating to the new consciousness can be fed in. All this can be achieved if we are sincere in our practice and move along with awareness.

The Vibro-Magnetic Breath will become a great delight to you as time goes on. This Breath is truly an 'electrical' breath. This cannot be explained, the feeling will come only with practise. A few weeks' practise will reveal much.

The Eight Spiritual Breaths

Posture for the Vibro-Magnetic Breath

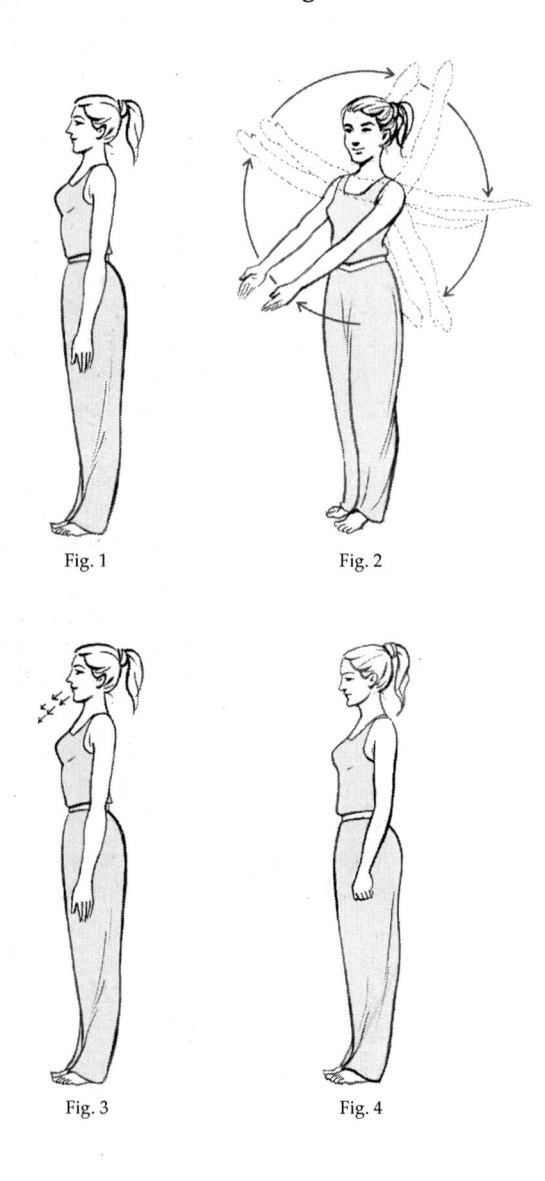

Fig. 1

Fig. 2

Fig. 3

Fig. 4

Note: This Breathing Exercise is powerful. Please follow the instructions carefully.

The Vibro-Magnetic Breath

Practising the Vibro-Magnetic Breath

Commence with two breaths; gradually increase to seven breaths over one or two weeks.

Stand erect as in the previous Breathing Exercise but with your arms at your sides. See that your spine is straight, buttocks tight and feet firmly on the ground.

1. Inhale a complete, deep breath. Retain the breath.

2. Keeping the body rigid from the soles of your feet to the top of your head, swing the arms and hands in a complete circle three times i.e. raise your arms to chest level, take them straight up over the head and back, and around again to the original position, before bringing them down. Repeat this motion three times.

3. At the third swing, drop the arms to the sides, exhaling 'shhhhhhh' vigorously through the mouth, but not relaxing the chest. This is one count.

At the seventh and final count inhale and relax, mentally repeating the spiritual Affirmation for this Breath as given on the following page.

Affirmation and Visualisation

The Ajna chakra retrieving a memory from the vault of the past.

To be memorised:

"Now, that liquid feeling in the body is spreading everywhere… relaxing me entirely.

"I am thinking of the loveliest thing I have ever known. There it comes: that beautiful picture, perhaps from long ago and far away – but there it is, perfectly clear before my mind, as if it happened just but a moment ago.

"I thank you Lord – I thank you, Law – for my memory.

"I thank you for helping me bring back from the vault of my past, a thing of beauty that is in my memory; (after reciting this, close the fist of your right hand tightly so that the happy memory is locked in. Now continue the Affirmation and, at the same time, try hard with your left hand to push negative thoughts, unsuccessfully, inside the tightly closed right fist). *I vow that from this moment onward, no negative thought of any kind will enter my memory. No thought of disease, decay, senility, old age, disappointment, doubt, failure, death.* (Now loosen the tight grip of your right fist and see that the fingers of the left hand slide into the loosened fist, as you continue with the Affirmation.) *Nothing will enter my memory but that which is in unison with all that is good and my very own, highest conception of truth. And there I see the whole conduct of humankind – there I see my whole conduct!*

"*Now, feeling happy and giving thanks, I once again will to see that picture lost in the absorption of my being, as I take a little breath and a long, deep, sweeping sigh.*

"*I now take another little breath and a quick sigh.*"

Effect of the Breathing Exercise and Affirmation

As you keep moving from one Breathing Exercise to the next, you keep the already awakened chakras active and energised while simultaneously activating the next chakra. While energising the Sahasrar centre and the Ajna, Vishuddhi and Anahat chakras – this Breath is designed to activate the Manipur chakra. By the time you have mastered these Breaths and their Affirmations, you have fully cleared the above chakras of all their toxins and are free to assimilate the knowledge that you have been accumulating through the Affirmations. If your practice has been regular and sincere, the results should have begun manifesting in some form or another, although you may not yet be aware of it. In due course, your meditations will bring to your awareness the transformation that is taking place within you.

You will notice that in this exercise, you swing your arms to the count of three each time you do the breath. What is the purpose of this? If you are doing your practice regularly and in the required manner, a great deal of energy would be created by this time and released by the energised chakras into the meridians. In order that any excess energy does not congest the subtle body and the auric field thus creating discomfort in the physical body, this energy needs to be dispersed. The swinging arms, while enhancing the activity of the chakra, also help in balancing this energy, making our journey simpler and free of any unwanted disorder.

The Eight Spiritual Breaths

Ajna chakra

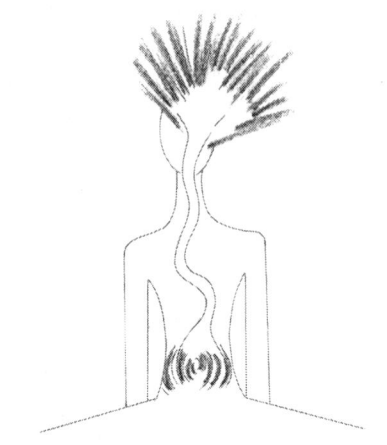

Free movement of energy between the Ajna, Vishuddhi, Anahat and Manipur chakra.

Once you start on your daily practise of the Breathing Exercises, you are re-energising all the chakras. The focus of the first five Breaths is on the Sahasrar, Ajna, Vishuddhi and Anahat chakras. So, while cleansing all the chakras, the Breaths continue to enhance to perfection the activity of the Sahasrar, Ajna and Vishuddhi chakras.

Once the Ajna chakra is developed, it becomes the witnessing centre. In other words, an aspirant becomes the detached observer of all events within the body and mind. He develops an awareness wherein he begins to 'see' the hidden essence underlying all that is visible.

> *"When Ajna is awakened, the meaning and significance of symbols flash into one's conscious perception, and intuitive knowledge arises effortlessly and one becomes a 'seer'."*
>
> – Swami Satyananda Saraswati

The visual on the previous page shows that the Breaths we have been practising have enabled the free movement of consciousness between the Ajna and Manipur chakras.

With the mastering of the first five Breaths, the descending energy has completed its purpose of clearing the passage for the free flow of energy between the Sahasrar centre and the four chakras. This means that there is no chance of energy getting trapped in these chakras.

Manipur chakra

The Manipur chakra is the centre of dynamism, energy, will power and achievement, and it is often compared to the dazzling heat of the sun. Just as the sun radiates energy and heat to support life on earth, in the same way the Manipur chakra radiates and distributes energy to the whole body. Balance to this chakra is brought through selfless service without the desire for reward. The practise of charity will clarify one's path of action or *karma*.

Meditation on this chakra awakens intensity and passion that is essential for sound health and physical power. Once consciousness ascends through the Manipur chakra and moves freely back and forth between the Ajna chakra and Manipur chakra, one can become the Master of one's life situations. Its element is fire (sight) and the sense organ is the eye.

Vibration of the expanded Manipur chakra.

The Vishuddhi and Manipur chakras working in unison.

The free flow of energy between the four chakras above indicates that the individual consciousness at the esoteric level and the mundane level is now equipped to handle any situation in a balanced state of being. The essence of opposites is transcended and consciousness has moved away from ill will, spite, hatred, greed, jealousy and judgement.

Breathing consciously will always dilate the meridians and release the data embedded in them. Remember, the subconscious data banks are not in the brain. They are distributed throughout the meridian system. When you focus on breathing, your dualistic data surfaces and with directed thinking in the form of Affirmations, we create balance and our awareness expands.

With the free flow of energy, past, stored memories at all the above levels of the chakras are released and all blocks dissolved. Many issues are sorted with the result that if these issues are manifesting as physical problems, they get healed; fears and insecurities are resolved. You suddenly discover the reasons for certain situations that you find yourself in, which in your right mind you would not get into. You now see this as a part of *karmic* residue that had to be resolved. The situations don't change; you have changed and view the same situation from a balanced point of view and awareness.

The Vibro-Magnetic Breath

With the balance of these chakras, we have achieved:

Simplicity: This is the mental dimension. It implies one-pointedness and focus that is essential to balance in this dimension.

Patience: This is the physical dimension. It implies relaxation and the absence of stress that is essential to balance in this dimension.

Compassion: This is the emotional dimension. It implies contentment and love as a shareable experience, which is essential to balance in this dimension.

"Without balance within these three dimensions, multi-dimensional actualisation is impossible. The trinity of the Physical, Emotional and Mental Dimensions are the densest of our dimensions where consciousness is most obscured. If we are not dedicated in our practice and do not bring these into balance, meditative mastery is not possible. Once they come to balance, then the subtler dimension of witness consciousness opens up as a detached observer and then, we are watching the physical, mental and emotional dimensions from the now dominant, subtle dimension of witness consciousness. The subtle dimension becomes more dominant in meditation. There is complete detachment from all levels of mental dimension and then, there is just the observation of stillness."

– Master Charles Cannon

Sit still, very peaceful and happy. Get into the habit of listening within. Do not strain. Success depends upon absolute relaxation.

With the completion of the five Breaths, you have completed the process of accessing the Descending Energy. You must be experiencing changes within yourself. There will be more awareness; you will be feeling lighter in body and mind. Some of you might be sensing, feeling and seeing the process of your growth.

Chapter Fourteen

6. The Cleansing Breath

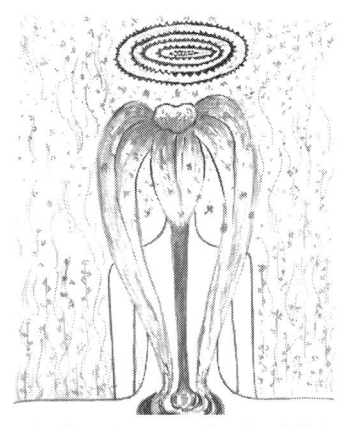

The Cleansing, Ascending Kundalini.

This is one of the most important Breaths because it leads us into the next phase of our growth – towards accessing the Ascending Energy. A lot of care has to be given to the practice and one has to be alert to the feeling it generates. With regular and diligent practise, you have cleansed and purified your chakras and all the negative data has been thrown out so that the energy released with this Breath will move up smoothly. With the Breathing Exercises and their relevant Affirmations you have cleared your subtle body meridians; you have expanded and invigorated the flow of your breath by dispersing the fear-ridden data stored in the body-mind organism. With the process of inhalation and vigorous exhalation, you have been rid of the feelings of anxiety, self-conflict and self-doubt. So, start practising the Cleansing Breath with full confidence.

The Eight Spiritual Breaths

Posture for the Cleansing Breath

Fig. 1

Fig. 2

Fig. 3

Fig. 4

Fig. 5

Fig. 6

Note: This Breathing Exercise is powerful. Please follow the instructions carefully.

The Cleansing Breath

Practising the Cleansing Breath

With this Breath you will be entering the second phase of your journey into self-discovery. This is a powerful phase where Kundalini will be activated and if you have been dedicated in your practise of the Spiritual Breaths, the energy should move smoothly.

Commence with two breaths; gradually increase to seven breaths over one or two weeks.

Stand erect as before. Buttocks tight. Feet firm on the ground. Feet level, ankles firm, calves tight, knees snapped back, thighs firm, buttocks firm and, most importantly, spine straight.

1. With the body perfectly straight, place the rigid arms with the palms overlapping each other and the thumbs crossed, as far behind the back as possible. Inhale a complete breath (you will have the feeling that the expanding chest is 'pulling' the arms apart). Keep the buttocks and legs firm.

2. When every air space in the chest is filled gradually unlock the hands without relaxing a single muscle; slowly bring the rigid arms to the sides, hands pointing downwards. Be sure that buttocks are tight.

3. Raise the arms and hands firmly in front with a sense of pulling the shoulders. Take them straight up over the head and around again to the original position. Do this three times, without allowing any breath to escape, and keeping the body rigid. Make sure that you complete three swings – holding the arms parallel, bringing them to the front, then up above the head, and back to position.

4. Bring the arms to the sides, standing firmly, and exhale 'shhhhhhh' vigorously through the mouth. After the seventh and final count inhale and relax, mentally repeating the spiritual Affirmation for this Breath. Of all the Breaths, this Breath is the most efficacious for the serious student – to feel and to direct the finer currents within him.

Affirmation and Visualisation

The fire of Divine love engulfing the body.

To be memorised:

(As you feel completely relaxed after this Breathing Exercise, mentally repeat the following Affirmation in a deep, devotional attitude of mind. While reciting it, you must do the action with your hands of taking the fire up from the base of the spine, moving it higher upwards, and then outwards. You are to strictly follow what you are instructed to do. There is a purpose to it.)

"I now feel a great heat at the base of my spine... it is moving up... up... up.

"I imagine a bright light that comes from the flame, which comes from the fire, which gives the heat... the fire of the Divine love within me. It's going up and out... up and out... up and out... it strikes the surface of the body... it seems to go beyond the body... up and out... up and out.

"I think of the top of my head and I see my whole body is full of light... light... light... the Light of Divine wisdom that is in every living thing.

"Now, ever so gently, not letting myself know it, I take a little breath and a long, deep, sweeping sigh. I now take another little breath and a quick sigh."

The Cleansing Breath

Explanation and importance of the first and sixth Breath

In the Memory Development Breath i.e. the first Breath, you have accessed the light of creative wisdom coming from the light of Divine love from above. This love is not based on selfish give-and-take love. Divine love is the love of God or the Creative Intelligence that maintains balance and harmony in the universe.

In the Cleansing Breath you are emphasising the reverse; the Affirmation says, 'the fire of Divine love'. This fire rises from Muladhar chakra at the base of the spine, where the Kundalini is lying dormant. It rises and you are made aware of the heat moving up the body. Then the Affirmation says, "...a bright light that comes from the flame, which comes from the fire, which gives the heat... the fire of the Divine love within me. It's going up and out..." This fire is not going to burn you because you have already accessed the fire of Divine love and wisdom through the practise of the Memory Development Breath. Taking it upwards and outwards, you are pouring Divine love on the whole earth.

Another aspect of the Kundalini's cleansing process.

The Eight Spiritual Breaths

Effect of the Breathing Exercise and Affirmation

If you have been regular with the practise of the last five Breaths and their Affirmations, then you are more or less ready to start on the path of the Ascending Energy. Being ready means that you have reached a state where you can maintain a balanced mind in the face of mental and emotional conflicts. It means that you can endure anger, worry, love and passion, disappointment, jealousies, hatred, memories of past sufferings and sorrow. If you have reached such a state, then you are ready for the awakening. If you do not have a guru, invoke internal guidance and proceed.

This is important because when the Ascending Energy is set in motion, it will start shaking all your illusions, your scripting, your deepest fears, insecurities, attachments and patterns developed over lifetimes. It will start shaking the conditioning, not only of the individual, but also the conditioning of the collective consciousness.

By following the course of the Descending Energy and having travelled down the chakras, a gradual transformation has taken place that has prepared your body-mind organism to receive the Ascending Energy in awareness and with full confidence. What was earlier viewed as complex will now be viewed as simple.

The practice that you are doing is to help you to remember your connection with your Self. Hopefully, you are practising at a fixed time, on a light stomach in an open space, or in front of a window, wearing loose clothing. This is stressed because you create a certain vibration at the place of your practice and meditation, which is of immense benefit as you go along.

Muladhar chakra

With the sixth Breath and Affirmation, we are activating the Muladhar chakra located at the base of the spine, at the perineum. Kundalini lies coiled here. Its element is earth, and the sense organ is the nose (smell). All psychic fragrances (fragrance that only an aspirant may experience) manifest here. It is the base from which the Ida, Pingala and Sushumna nadis emerge. When Ida and Pingala are purified, then an awakening is sparked off here that arouses the Kundalini. All the passions, guilt and agonies are stored here. In order to get rid of the guilt and neurosis, the shakti needs to move out of this chakra. Physiologically, it is related to the excretory, urinary, sexual and reproductive organs.

Atoms and Cells

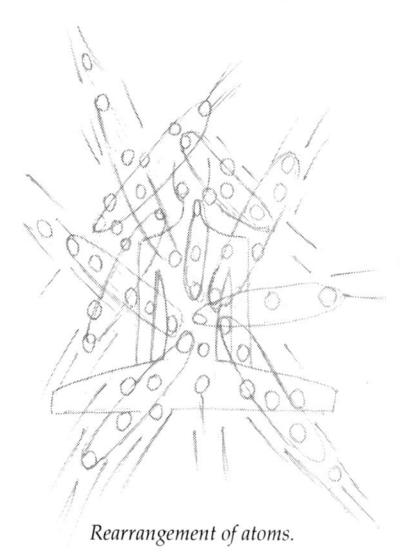

Rearrangement of atoms.

Once the Ascending Energy moves up, the atoms that are the subtle building blocks for the physical form get agitated and start moving about at random like ping-pong balls which you may sense, see or feel. This process goes on during meditation till they get rearranged in a new pattern. Just like the atoms, the cells also rearrange themselves and as new understanding dawns, we realise how ignorant we were earlier.

The human body is made is made up of millions of cells that complement each other and function as a harmonious whole in the body. Each cell carries the genetic coding and is empowered to create skin, bones, hair, etc. that comprise our physical bodies.

Dispersion of cells.

These cells are storehouses of information that has been gained over lifetimes and they are in a constant state of growth and renewal. Just as our breath can be left to automatically function or be consciously directed by our awareness, so also our cells can be consciously influenced by our intention.

You can direct the power that is within every cell through the intention of your thoughts and feelings. This is the process of transformation. The upheaval is natural and necessary to facilitate the process of balancing the body-mind organism in order to access and understand the knowledge.

Faith

What is 'faith'? Osho tells us, "When you cannot prove something but still believe in it – that is faith. Faith is not intellectual, it is not a concept; it is a jump into the impossible, the unknown. When you have come to a point from where you have stretched reason to its logical extreme, you have come to a point that reason cannot go beyond – then what? You know that there is existence beyond a point where reason ends, so what do you do? If your curiosity wants to know what is beyond, you have to take the jump – a quantum leap." In common terms, taking the quantum leap means taking a risk, going off into uncharted territory without a guide. It also means risking something that no one else would risk.

Chapter Fifteen

7. The Grand Rejuvenation Breath

What you have been following is a fully-developed system of scientific, spiritual Breathing Exercises to guide the breath through various stages of healing and transformation. This is achieved at all levels of our mental, emotional and physical being. If the instructions are not followed diligently and the sequence is not maintained (the Breaths lock into each other), it can produce uncomfortable side-effects at the mental, emotional and physical levels.

The Affirmation of this Breath gives you an indication of the level of healing capacity you have gained. You have to direct your breath and attention to the problem area in your body, and depending on how you have developed – you can heal yourself.

Sometimes, it may happen that an aspirant finds certain Breaths difficult to master. This is alright. The idea is not to rush in or force oneself to do it. Go slow and steady and in due course it will happen. One aspirant found the second Breath, the Revitalisation Breath, difficult to master whereas I found the Grand Rejuvenation Breath difficult. It took me almost a year to do the required number of seven Breaths. Please understand – the full and perfect mastery of a Breath is a long process, so be patient.

The Eight Spiritual Breaths

Posture for the Grand Rejuvenation Breath

Fig. 1   Fig. 2   Fig. 3   Fig. 4

Fig. 5   Fig. 6   Fig. 7   Fig. 8

Note: This Breathing Exercise is powerful. Please follow the instructions carefully.

The Grand Rejuvenation Breath

Practising the Grand Rejuvenation Breath

Commence with two breaths; gradually increase to seven breaths over one or two weeks.

This is a relatively difficult breath compared to the earlier ones and will take some time to reach the required number of seven.

Stand erect as in the previous exercise. See that the spine is straight, buttocks tight and feet firm on the ground.

1. Place hands on the hips, gripping tightly. Inhale a complete breath. Keep elbows forward. Shoulders must not be raised; they must be down and not as an anchor.

2. See that the legs and buttocks are stiff. Then, bend the neck as far forward and downward as you can without relaxing in any way. There will be a pulling sensation from the neck and the bottom of the spine. Then come back to your original position. Do this three times. (After a little practise, you will be able to do this in a rhythmic way with no difficulty in holding of your breath.)

3. Standing perfectly erect, exhale evenly but vigorously, letting out all the air in the body through the mouth (as in all the exercises). Do not inhale, but bend forward from the waist, then backward as far as possible, forward again and backward, three times. This is one count. After the seventh count, stand rigidly erect and still, inhale and relax, mentally repeating the spiritual Affirmation for this Breath.

Affirmation and Visualisation

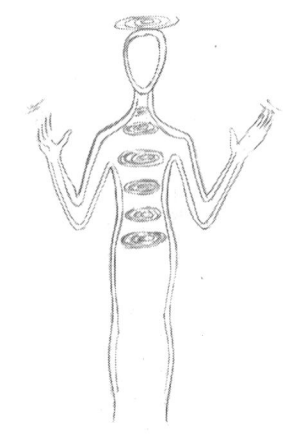

Affirming youthfulness in all its aspects.

Bring life and joy into your voice and action as you recite the Affirmation.

To be memorised:

"The success of this breath depends entirely upon my ability to relax. I relax entirely. I feel happy all over.

"I am youth! I am youth! Glorious youth, wonderful youth, radiant and vibrant youth, fearless, achieving, daring, conquering youth... full of courage, strength and power!

"I thought my body wore out and grew old like an old pair of shoes, but now I know, as I stand in the Presence, that new cells are being made for me... I am being renewed!

"I sing the Song of Conquest – there is no age for me, no decay, no disease, no senility – no death. I am free... free from the ravages of time, free from all negation of my own mind. I am free – young, young! I am glad. I rejoice. I am young forevermore!

"Now, feeling happy and giving thanks, I take a little breath and a long, deep, sweeping sigh. Now, I take another little breath and a quick sigh."

Effect of the Breathing Exercise and Affirmation

The healing energy that goes up the body in the Grand Rejuvenation Breath from the Muladhar through the Swadhisthan, Manipur, Anahat and Vishuddhi chakras, purifies the organs related to the chakras along the way. With this process, transformation takes place and we are renewed in body and mind. Old atoms have been rearranged and renewed. The old order of cells has dispersed and has settled into a new pattern, bringing with it a new understanding and a new way of being.

Ajna and Swadhisthan chakras working in unison.

The movement of the chakras may not be felt because by now they would have performed their role of breaking the blocks and clearing the path for Kundalini to move freely. They will come into play only when necessary i.e. if circumstances create any resistance or further blocks. Otherwise, when one has transformed from the old pattern of being, these two chakras – the Ajna and Swadhisthan – help the aspirant to maintain balance between the spiritual and mundane life.

This will lead towards the creation of a 'new you'.

In the Swadhisthan chakra, desires and fantasies of a sexual nature can be a problem. Instead of standing alone, an individual moves towards forming relationships and reaches out to family and friends for physical contact. In the brain, this chakra is represented by the unconscious mind. All our karmas are stored in this chakra. Restlessness and confusion are its characteristics. However, once purified, this chakra encompasses the astral plane as well as freedom from feelings and emotions of fantasy, jealousy, mercy, envy and joy.

In the Grand Rejuvenation Breath, with the movement of the head, we are consciously bringing down the Descending Energy and activating the Ajna and Vishuddhi chakras. Then bending forward and backward, we are stroking the Ascending Energy to move up. The purpose is to help both energies to meet at the central point – the Manipur chakra. This balances the mental, emotional and physical bodies by increasing creativity, self-control, sensitivity and responsibility towards family and social norms, as well as solidarity with the surrounding world.

The organs that are exercised in the process are the thyroid gland, liver, pancreas and the abdominal organs.

Balance

Expansion of the etheric body in all directions from the Manipur chakra.

The Grand Rejuvenation Breath

"At the navel region, there is an important junction where two vital forces, Prana and Apana meet. The Prana moves up and down between the navel and throat, and the Apana flows up and down between the perineum and navel. These two movements are normally coupled together, like two railway carriages, so that with the inspired breath, Prana is experienced moving up from the navel to the throat, while Apana is simultaneously moving up to the navel center from mooladhara. Then with exhalation, Prana descends from the throat to the navel and Apana descends from the manipura to mooladhara. In this way Prana and Apana are continually functioning together and changing direction with the flow of the inspired/expired breath."

– Swami Niranjanananda Saraswati

In earlier times, an aspirant who wished to travel on the spiritual path had to spend seven years or more in order to first gain balance in the physical, mental and emotional dimensions before being initiated into meditation. Each of these primary dimensions had a practice assigned to it. These practices were *Bhakti Yoga* – path of devotion, to bring balance to the emotional dimension; *Jnana Yoga* – path of knowledge, to bring balance to the mental dimension; and *Karma Yoga* – path of service, to bring balance to the physical dimension. It was determined that these three dimensions could be brought into balance over a period of seven years. Then followed the initiation into meditation that focused on the more subtle dimensions. During this period, an actual shift takes place and if you are aware, you can experience the changes taking place in the subtle bodies by either seeing the shift happening, or feeling a shift in the vibrations.

In the figure on the next page, you can see the etheric left brain that extends and moves into the open mouth flower-like bell of the right brain. This is the activity of the Ajna chakra.

The Eight Spiritual Breaths

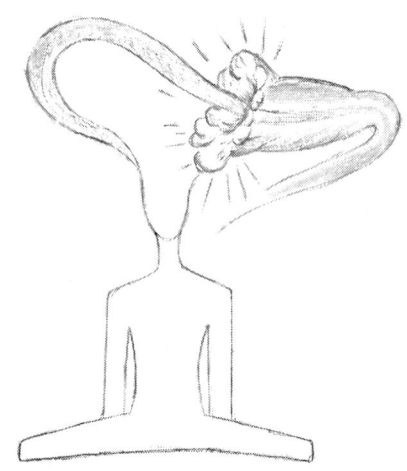

The left-brain merges with the right brain bringing into balance both the hemispheres.

When you have reached this state of balance, you become the witness of whatever experience you are creating for yourself. You can transform imbalance into balance. You have a choice. As balance occurs, the negative merges into the positive. The field of opposites dissolves. One reaches the understanding that nothing is good or bad; there is no right and wrong. Everything is, as is.

With the right and left-brain merging, the two polarities, that is the right and left hemisphere of the brain, work in synchronicity.

Chapter Sixteen

8. Your Own Spiritual Breath

You have come a long way in your practice and would have now realised that you can consciously breathe with awareness and control, or you can breathe unconsciously. Swami Niranjanananda Saraswati tells us that, "If the breath is unconscious, it falls under the control of primitive parts of the brain, where emotions, thoughts and feelings of which we have little or no awareness become involved. In this way the regularity and rhythm of the breath are disturbed and it flows in an uncoordinated way, creating havoc in the body and mind."

If you have become sensitive to the flow of Prana through the Eight Breathing Exercises, you may have become aware of more subtle levels of existence. The mastery of a Breath and its related Affirmation, the feeling or sensation it invokes, would be an indication to the way you are progressing. This would happen only if you have been very aware and finely tuned to your practice; always alert to any sensation that arises, relaxing into it so that it completes itself. Once you become comfortable in the practice, learn to be aware and observe through which chakra you are inhaling and exhaling.

If you have not noticed this so far, then I suggest you bring awareness to your Breaths as you perform them. This will further enhance the process.

The Eight Spiritual Breaths

Posture for Your Own Spiritual Breath

Fig. 1

Fig. 2

Fig. 3

Fig. 4

Fig. 5

Note: This Breathing Exercise is powerful. Please follow the instructions carefully.

Practising Your Own Spiritual Breath

Commence with two breaths; gradually increase to seven breaths over one or two weeks.

Stand erect and see that the spine is perfectly straight. Feet should be well apart and firm on ground (this is the only exercise with feet apart).

1. Inhale a complete breath through the nostrils and retain it.

2. Place hands on the hips as in the last exercise. Now, standing rigid, bend the body to the right as far as you can. Then, without any jerking movement, bend over as far as you can to the left. Do this three times.

3. This must be done slowly and rhythmically. On the completion of the third movement, with hands still gripping the hips, exhale 'shhhhhhh' vigorously through the mouth. This is one count.

4. After the seventh count inhale and relax, mentally repeating the spiritual Affirmation for this Breath as given on the following page.

Affirmation and Visualisation

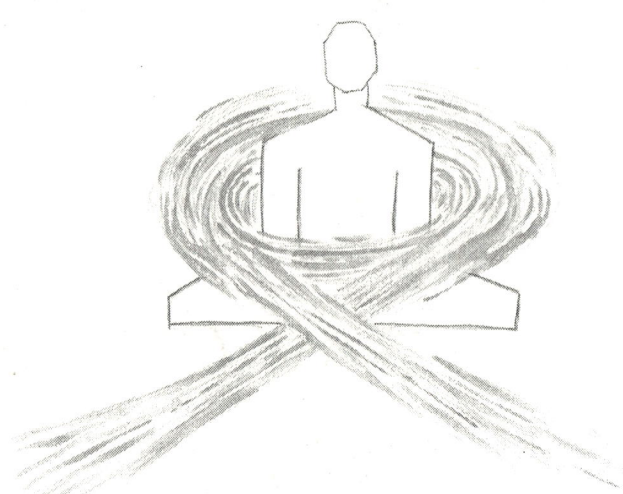

The guru's vibrations move out to enfold all aspirants.

To be memorised:

"I am now thinking upwards to the top of my head. I am thinking joy, joy, joy! And now, at the same time, I send it out! Out! Out!

"I embrace all in the practice of Brahma Vidya wherever they may be. I embrace the city... I embrace the state... and now I see great waves of light rolling out, growing of their own accord, wave upon wave, upon wave. I embrace the country...

"I embrace the whole world (imagine you are embracing a huge globe). *I embrace the whole human race. And now, with the Light of the Divine wisdom within me, with my love, with my joy and with my life... I embrace every living thing.*

"I now stand firm in case the light is too strong for me as it returns to me, not from the one point from which I send it, but from all the points. It is coming back... nearer... nearer... nearer... and now it embraces me, it embosses me, it overwhelms me. That Light of the Divine wisdom, that love, that joy, that life that comes to me from every living thing, so that I see my whole body, this wide universe, full of light, light, light!

"And now, I will charge every cell in my physical body with the Light of the Divine wisdom, that love, that joy, that life that comes to me from every living thing. Giving thanks and feeling happy, I take a little breath and a long, deep, sweeping sigh.

"Now I lock that light up within me, as I take another little breath... and a quick sigh."

Accessing the solar force through the worship of the sun.

This Breath further activates the Swadhisthan and Muladhar chakra.

"Swadhisthana is the storehouse of mental impressions. 'It is said that all the karmas, the past lives, the previous experiences, the greater dimension of the human personality that is unconscious, can be symbolized by Swadhisthana chakra. This chakra is the storehouse of mental impressions and karmas collected over lifetimes. It is the home of the unconscious'."

– Swami Satyananda Saraswati

Muladhar chakra is the seat of Kundalini, where it is lying dormant like a coiled serpent.

"In Mooladhara, the karmas of the lower stages of our evolution are manifested in the form of anger, greed, jealousy, passion, love, hate and so on."

– Swami Niranjanananda Saraswati

Chapter Seventeen

Wisdom gained through the Breaths

Wisdom gained through the Breaths

You have come a long way in your practice and by this time you would be going through your own experiences. Most of the old data would have been replaced by new data through the Affirmations. As mentioned earlier, the last three Breaths are designed to expel embedded data in the lower chakras.

Once you have mastered all the Breaths and Affirmations along with the Meditational Affirmations that are in the next chapter, you will have moved towards transformation at the mental, emotional and physical levels. You will have moved away from the race-mind. You will not accept tradition received from previous generations without independent personal thought on it. Only after subjecting it to critical examination, profound reflection, and after adding the result of your own understanding to it will you pass it on to humanity at large, thus becoming a factor for the higher evolution of mankind.

The Breathing Exercises, Affirmations and Meditation become a part of your life and daily practice. If done with the most reverential attitude, you will gradually move on to the inner regions of light. In your meditations, you will witness the light and you will know that your body is 'Light'. Absolute faith and regularity in your Breathing Exercises will reward you adequately.

Mind

Based on its functional aspects, the mind is divided into two parts. These are usually referred to as the left and the right brain hemispheres. The left is the objective mind or the conscious mind; the mind you use for your day-to-day life. The conscious mind acts as a guard to the subconscious mind. It is only with the consent of the conscious mind that any information can filter down to the subconscious mind.

There are four stages to the mind:

1. **Ordinary thinking:** When the mind moves at random from one thought to another.
2. **Contemplation**: When we give the mind a direction and formulate a course of action, and our thoughts are no longer fragmented. Contemplation is rational and logical.
3. **Concentration:** When the mind is not allowed to move; it is only allowed to stay in one point, at one place.
4. **Meditation:** When one becomes a witness to one's thoughts. Ultimately meditation is a state of no-mind. It becomes the 'Silent Observer'.

The right brain comprises the subjective mind or the subconscious mind. It is also called the unconscious mind. The subconscious mind looks after your involuntary system. The beat of your heart, the circulation of the blood, the function of your liver, kidneys; in fact all your vital organs and the cells unknown to you are controlled by the subconscious mind. Despite its perfection, it does not have the faculty of reasoning though its power is far more than the conscious mind. Once any information goes into the subconscious mind, it gets stored forever and is never forgotten. A simple example is running down the stairs. After the first few steps, the action is carried forward automatically; once swimming or cycling is learned, it is registered in the subconscious. So, it is imperative that the conscious mind be alert at every step in order to be always on guard as to what passes through to the unconscious. This would require constant awareness in our daily living. In Brahma Vidya, we are consciously feeding in positive data to replace the conditioned, stored data through the Affirmations and becoming Masters of our destiny, thus moving towards conscious competence.

Thought

The definite purpose of the Breathing Exercises and Affirmations is to slowly and steadily decondition the conditioned mind, to change the process of thought. Though a thought cannot be seen or handled or tasted, yet the influence of thought produces an effect that exactly corresponds to it. According to the power of our thought, we develop the energy and attract the substance necessary for the thought to manifest. Our thinking makes us what we are. Our thinking makes us do what we do. And our thinking makes everything in our life what it is. In other words, our life – all that we do and say and feel – will be in correspondence with our thought.

Emotions

All our emotions manifest at the level of thought and are felt through the body. Emotions are closely related to thought. In fact, they arise out of thought and whether we are aware or not, they have an affect on the body for good or ill.

For example, we all know that when we are excited, our heart beats faster; when we experience embarrassment, we blush or feel a hot flush or become tense with anger or fear. Yet, we are not conscious that our emotions are affecting our body every moment that we live. The emotions that are repetitive, or the ones we dwell on most, get deeply rooted and become the content of our moods. These moods become so firmly rooted in our minds that we become unconscious of them and don't realise that they affect our life.

Like the magnet having a negative and positive pole, emotions move in two directions. The positive is that of attraction or love, and the negative is that of repulsion or hate.

Some of the positive qualities of love are: wisdom, knowledge, benevolence, innocence, fearlessness, happiness, joy, youth, faith, health, strength, etc.

Some of the negative qualities of hate are: ignorance, vice, guilt, fear, sorrow, cowardice, grief, worry, sadness, revenge, selfishness, doubt, etc.

These are but a few of the emotions and they can be further divided and sub-divided. For example, fear becomes anxiety, misgiving, gloom and so on. All negative emotions are destructive and cause harm at all levels to the human body. In the meditations, you are emphasising the positive principles of love so that these get established consciously in the conscious mind by persistent meditation. Once that is done, you are no longer fooled by the illusion of the senses because then you know the Truth of who you are and what you are.

Spleen

With Your Own Spiritual Breath, the work of the Spleen is enhanced. With the clearing, the spleen accesses the solar life-principle that is constantly poured into the earth's atmosphere by the sun, and processes it into Prana.

Spleen assimilating solar energy in the form of pink coloured globules.

The Eight Spiritual Breaths

> *"The brilliant minute, vitality globules each consisting of seven physical atoms are charged with prana. When the globule is flashing in the atmosphere, brilliant as it is, it is almost colourless and shines with a white or slightly golden light. But as soon as it is drawn into the vortex (force-centre) of a chakra, it is decomposed and breaks up into different colours. As its component atoms are whirled round the vortex, each of the spokes of the chakra seizes one of them, so that all the atoms charged with yellow flow along one, and all those charged with green flow along another, and so on. The rose-coloured ray runs all over the body along the nerves, and is the life of the nervous system. If the nerves are not sufficiently supplied with this rosy light a person would become sensitive and extremely irritable. A person in robust health usually absorbs so much more of this vitality than what is actually needed by his own body that he is constantly radiating a torrent of rose-coloured atoms and once assimilated by the body it gives a luminous, pink glow of life and health to the body."*
>
> – C. W. Leadbeater

By the time you reach the Eighth Breath, your whole system becomes very light and sensitive. If you have been regular in your practice, you may be sensing or feeling a state of expansion.

Chapter Eighteen

A Healthy Mind in a Healthy Body

Training the Subconscious Mind

As you go along, you will know that the subconscious mind believes what it is told without question, and it immediately sets to work to build the temple according to the principles that you will claim for it. And, no matter what your directions may be, the result is bound to materialise, for the subconscious mind accepts without question what you tell it or the instructions you give.

The Breaths and the Affirmations help you understand what life is, what the origin of life is, and what it is that causes life. For this understanding to arise, one not only needs a healthy mind but also a healthy body. Mind-power can do almost anything, provided it has the right instrument and material to work through. Thought alone cannot keep a starving man from getting weak, nor can it maintain the health of a person who does not provide his body with the important elements it needs.

The Creative Intelligence within must be given the substance with which to build a capable brain and body. This substance consists of five nourishments: solid food, liquid food, rest, breath and thought. Each of the five must be the right kind, and all five are required to build a gloriously strong and capable individual. Thought can work wonders, but not without the other four essential nourishments. What is lacking most in our lives is the sufficient quantity of breath. If there is such a thing as food for the brain, it is breath.

Meditating with Focus

As regards meditation, it must be noted that meditation without focus is of little use. Meditation of a lazy, dreamy or wandering mind does more harm than good. Any affirmation done without proper attention to the words will send a garbled message to the subconscious, resulting in a confused result. Sometimes, we face situations which make no sense to us and we wonder what the purpose of the whole thing was. It is the result of unclear messages we are sending to the subconscious mind.

The power of focus, of putting force behind our thoughts (intense feeling) and words can only be learned through practise. The most effective practices known are being given to you in the practices of the Breaths and Affirmations. It first requires a strong urge to discover the Truth, followed by a considerable amount of practise, as well as concentration for any length of time on one thought, with every other thought and sensation shut out before real silence and peace are attained.

If you are regular and dedicated in your practice to discover the power that is working within you and for you, rest assured that it will be made known to you. It may take a little longer for you than with others, but it will come, as long as you persevere and stay peaceful and happy. Practise calmness in your speech, a calmness that embodies conviction and control. Let every word that you utter convey your thought perfectly and appropriately.

To give an example: During the course of my meditation I felt all energy leaving me. It was a scary feeling. I called my guru on the phone and told him that my brain was 'dead'. He insisted that I come up with the right word for what I was trying to convey. Because, if the brain were dead, how would I be talking? With much focus, I was made to come up with a correct word and repeat the sentence: "My brain is numb."

This incident made me very aware as to the careless way we live our lives and unknowingly send wrong messages to the subconscious mind, thus producing unwanted results.

You are now laying the foundation. Therefore, be of humble mind like a child and true knowledge will come to you faster. The Truth is very simple; it is in our constant questioning and debating that it keeps slipping from us. You are advised to drop all that you have learned so far and that has not been proven in the acid test of your own experience. There must be no conflict in your thinking. Just follow what you are being guided to do and everything will unfold gradually.

Understanding the Creative Principle

The whole universe and all that is in it, animate and inanimate, is governed by the immutable laws set by the Creative Intelligence. Your body is tuned to operate at a certain rhythm by the Creative Intelligence within, and once set in motion will continue to automatically perform its functions unless we interfere with it through over indulgence of our appetites. This same Creative Intelligence has set in rhythm and motion, the functioning of the animal and plant kingdom and the cycle of creation, dissolution and recreation for the universe, and it moves in clockwork fashion. The sun and the moon will not deviate from their role. Nature will keep moving according to immutable, imperishable laws set by the creative principle unless man interferes with them.

When you are in a garden or if you imagine you are there and you look around at the trees, the grass, the flowers, you see creativity everywhere. This creativity is never ceasing in its activity and knows its work absolutely. Isolate something, rest your mind upon it, see whether you can see why it is, what it is, and why it is doing what it does.

Consider any living thing, say, an apple tree. Don't you see? The apple tree knows how to make apples, and that is the only thing that knows how to make an apple, and that is universal with all apple trees. An oyster knows exactly how to build its shell and make the pearl. You may make an imitation but you cannot make a natural pearl. That is the way the course of nature follows. A human being is the only thing that can create another human being. Every living thing has the power to reproduce itself and continue the stream of life.

We might think that science is beginning to create life, but this is not exactly so. I recall a joke that explains this:

God is sitting in Heaven when a scientist says to Him, "Lord, we don't need you anymore. Science has finally figured out a way to create life out of nothing. In other words, we can now do what You did in the beginning."

"Oh, is that so? Tell me..." replies God.

"Well," says the scientist, "we can take dirt and form it into the likeness of You and breathe life into it, thus creating man."

"Well, that's interesting... show Me."

So the scientist bends down to the earth and starts to mold the soil.

"No, no, no..." interrupts God, "Get your own dirt."

As we look at this creative spirit, we see three things:

First: That it is intelligent.
Second: That it is present everywhere.
Third: That it is all-powerful.

Therefore, the creative spirit is:

Omniscient.
Omnipresent.
Omnipotent.

These three factors are present everywhere in the universe and comprise activity, which is the origin of all things.

Chapter Nineteen

Thought Forms

All thoughts come to us from without; therefore, we must treat thoughts as guests and not allow them to become hosts. When you hold a thought along a definite channel, it would be naive to accept any other result than what the thought would create. The appropriate method of dealing with thoughts is to observe them and let them pass!

Since my perception is best through visualisation, I am given ample proof as to why thoughts should not be allowed to build a permanent residence within us but allowed in only as visitors! I have seen that every thought that was fed into my mind immediately assumed a form. It stayed with me till I looked at it and acknowledged and addressed it before it moved out from my consciousness in the same form.

You can do a little exercise for yourself:

Think of any person, place or thing and then look into your mind. Do you see how your mind has created a form almost instantly? So, if these thoughts are not allowed to move out, what will happen is exactly what happens to a one-room apartment with twenty people occupying it. They will spill over into the doorway, into the passageway, down the stairway and into the compound. If you cling to your thoughts and do not release them, there is going to be clogging of the outlets and rot will start setting in as the plethora of thoughts jam your system.

Imagine hundreds of thought forms going 'yak-yak-yak' in your brain. You are bound to have a heavy head or a migraine!

If this form of energy starts putrefying, depending on the chakra it is related to, it is bound to cause an ulcer, tumour or just plain congestion. If not rationalised or worked out and released, this energy becomes a part of your consciousness as your chronic 'dis-ease', especially if it is a fatalistic or pessimistic thought.

If we do not live consciously, then we are allowing all and sundry thoughts to filter into the subconscious. I view the subconscious as a restricted operator in the sense that it has no discriminative power. It does not know the difference between good or bad, right and wrong. Its job is to produce results. How important is it then that the conscious mind stands as a sentinel to always be aware and alert to check everything that passes into the subconscious. This is what is going to create your future!

Imagine the subconscious to be like a big earthen pot. In the course of your life, you put some wheat into it, then some rice, then some rubble, then some gold and silver and again some dirt and so on. Now, this pot has a hole at the bottom. What is the order in which you receive what you have placed inside, and in what form?

As I said, the subconscious cannot discriminate: it only performs its duty of producing results. If, during the course of my conversation with a friend, I tell her, "You make me sick," or "You are a pain in the neck," these thought forms filter into the subconscious and produce their results in the course of time. That is certain! If, however, I am conscious of the power of thoughts, I would immediately replace my statement with, "I do not agree with your style of working," or, "This statement of yours is presenting a challenge to me," or something to that effect.

It is seen that what the conscious mind accepts and decides upon as true, the subconscious mind automatically accepts as true without judgement. The subconscious mind has no faculty of reason or judgement. Therefore, the conscious mind has to decide for it, but the subconscious mind has all the power to do whatever it is directed by the conscious mind to do. Here is an exercise which an aspirant is advised to practise for a week. This does not form the part of daily practice.

Every morning, during the week, you are asked to awaken a little earlier than is your normal practice. It would be ideal to freshen up and dress with particular care as if you are going to meet someone whose opinion you value; in other words, you are going to meet your Self. Then do the following:

- Stand before a mirror
- Smile at yourself with pleasure, looking squarely in the eyes
- Commence the following conversation with yourself: Call yourself by your own name i.e. "I, Ram Sharan…"

"I am deeply grateful to you, for I have learned that you are able to do whatever I wish to do. I have learned to place absolute trust in you."

(Be dramatic. Arouse your emotions. Smile with great pleasure and feel very happy.)

"My faith in you is unbounded, for all things are possible to you. I have learned that, 'You are what the Creator is'. I have discovered what the creative energy in you can do and it is wanting to do whatever I direct it to do."

(Look deep into your eyes and believe that what you are saying is true, true, true! Act as if you are on the verge of some great realisation of joy or success, or whatever you have in mind for yourself.)

"You are success. You will achieve today whatever you set out to achieve, for you have discovered the new power, for which there is nothing that is impossible."

(Rouse yourself to a high state of emotion. Let your eyes shine and look with earnest concentration in your eyes. Feel a warmth of love towards yourself and everybody, declaring that as you will expect, demand and receive help from others, so are you prepared to help others. Start out with this intention.

The Eight Spiritual Breaths

Be kind, smile at people and then watch, and you will be surprised how the response in others will be precisely in correspondence with your own attitude.)

So, with affirmations you are consciously putting yourself in the driver's seat by impressing your intention on the subconscious mind, because that is what is going to provide the energy, the force and lead what you affirm to fructification. It is simple to impress your thought on the subconscious mind, for whatever you tell it, it believes, because it does not have the faculty of reason.

You need to keep affirming them during the course of the day so that they become a part of your system and create their positive vibrations for you. With constant practise, you become watchful of what you say, and with awareness you re-programme your data bank and create a new you!

Chapter Twenty

Energy Blocks and Un-Ease

My visual journey in self-discovery has lent a very clear understanding of the human condition as a whole. Our very physical form and its appearance is the result of our thoughts. Once we become conscious of this and understand the game, we realise that all we need to do is imagine how we want to be and that is exactly how we shall be. We shall be self-created. As it is, we are following the rules of Creation, but are doing it unconsciously. There is no system to our thought flow. There is a constant inflow and outflow of random thoughts, most of which have no meaning in our life. We collect them and store them as junk data, thus causing congestion and traffic jams. The flow of energy becomes jammed, thus compelling it to find nooks and crevices through which it can manoeuvre its way so that we can go about our lives in a reasonable state of well-being. The best way to control the inflow of random thoughts would be to set the conscious mind as a censor to reactive thoughts, thus giving us an opportunity to act appropriately.

Un-ease before dis-ease? How does it set in and manifest itself?

When does un-ease and dis-ease set in? It is at times when we are not comfortable in any particular situation; when we are upset or our emotions have been disturbed through any negative feelings of hate, rejection, dejection, greed, revenge, resentment etc. If these negative emotions are not resolved and are harboured within our body-mind intellect, then in time, they start to slowly, steadily putrefy and solidify and we set the process of un-ease in motion, which would ultimately manifest as a disease in the physical body.

At first, the negative emotion (that takes the form of congealed energy resembling a black, jelly-like substance) will start clogging and thus obstruct the free flow of Prana in the subtle body meridians. This would be experienced as fluctuation of moods and imbalance in the trinity of physical, emotional and mental dimensions. If an individual is following any self-development programme, then through the process of meditation and self-analysis, he will be able to resolve/dissolve the negative emotion that has taken the form of clogged energy. In this way, through conscious living, we move towards spiritual growth and prevent the clogged emotion from further solidifying and obstructing the flow of Prana in the subtle body. This obstruction could lead to a lack of proper blood supply to the related organ, thus possibly leading to some form of disease.

The message is, "We are the Masters of our destiny and authors of our death." If we can live a happy, balanced life in harmony with the universal laws, without getting entangled in the inflow of random thoughts, we will probably move through life smoothly without causing an upheaval in the working of the system as a whole. Be calm, be cool, be non-judgemental, non-complaining and non-reactive. If you can follow these simple rules, then you are living in awareness. Remember the 'other' has nothing to do with us. We are each creating our own script and drama, choosing our own cast, and allotting the roles to each as befits our psyche and who we feel are suitable to help us move through our growth and karmic patterns. Therefore, more often than not, there is friction in the stimuli and response in human interaction, for each is operating from the pre-inscribed script in his/her psyche. So wake up and be in the Now, and don't live from past scripted patterns of stored data. Break your conditioning because it is hampering your growth. Learn to live consciously and in awareness; the endeavour always being to respond to a situation and not react to it. In due course this 'awareness' will come naturally to you and it will seem so simple.

Chapter Twenty One

Preparation for Meditation

Explanation

We see that the creative force pervades everywhere and everything. It is omniscient, omnipresent and omnipotent. There is not a single embodiment of life where this creative force is not in existence and it is the origin of all things. Let the truth of the above revelation sink within you, dwell on it, and contemplate the truth of your own life as well. Can you feel your imagination working? You may not have thought about this creativity that is universal, in this way before. Feel happy, for you will see that God as you have always visualised (whether as a being up above in some place called heaven, or in any other manner), is really the creative principle everywhere, as equally present and knowable. How you receive the knowledge that is being revealed to you depends on your intuition and power of thought. We now come to the understanding that the universe and God are not separate. We also realise that the created man and the Creator are not separate. "God is in man, and man is in God."

The following is to be read aloud to yourself, with feeling, memorised and added to the Meditational Affirmations:

The Eight Prayers:

"You, O Lord, who are the life and support of the universe, who are dearer than life, purify my head.

You, who are free from all pain, by coming into contact with whom I am freed from all troubles, purify my eyes.

You, who pervade the universe, directing and controlling it, purify my throat.

You, who are comprehending, purify my heart.

You, who are the cause of the universe, purify my body.

You, who are all-sustaining, purify my feet.

You, who are all-truth, purify again my head.

You, who are all-pervading, purify my whole organism."

Understanding of The Eight Prayers:

"You, O Lord, who are the life and support of the universe, who are dearer than life, purify my head."

What can be dearer than life? It can only be that which supports life and the universe, a force that is invisible but is the be all and end all of all creation. 'Purify my head' – because inside the head is located the means by which one receives thoughts and ideas from the universal mind, absorbs them and then, after processing them according to one's psyche, sends them out again. With the voiced request, you ask the Lord to purify your head, which is the centre of communication, so there will be right understanding of the universe and all its activities.

"You, who are free from all pain, by coming into contact with whom I am freed from all troubles, purify my eyes."

Since your mind is made up of the accumulation of ideas, have you ever stopped to think where these ideas come from? Most of them come to you through your eyes, and are false, but you believe them to be true. Invariably, most people do not simply see what they are looking at, but see it coloured by the beliefs of a conditioned mind. You might see someone you hold in high esteem, crossing the road with his arm around a woman you do not hold in high regard. Witnessing the scene, your mind passes a judgement and stores it in your memory. You do not stop to think of the circumstance that prompted the action. Maybe the woman was sick, or she had sprained her foot. We should pray that we store in our mind that which is right knowledge, so that our mind may grow in balance with the universal mind, and that on the spiritual plane of life we see with the inner eye.

"You, who pervade the universe, directing and controlling it, purify my throat."

Why the throat? The word is the sound of the universe. Your word is your power. But there is something that is more powerful than sound – and that is silence. We can only reach the silence and rest in it, when we properly understand and use sound. Every sound that can possibly be made by any living being in the universe comes from one sound – the 'Word of God' as some call it, and others call the 'First Vibration'.

The mind is impressed by sound more than by anything else, and the only way to reach soundlessness is through sound. Your sound emanates from the throat, and you have the will to choose that what comes out of your throat shall or shall not be in accordance with what you know to be the Truth. You are advised not to waste your energy in uttering useless sounds. As my guru taught me, it is wise to 'have no tongue'. If you keep what you know to yourself, it will generate great power within you. Use it only when you know that you are in contact with people who will benefit from your words. You may not get the meaning of this yet but, rest assured, it will come. Till then, you are asked to speak only when you have something worthwhile to say – no slander, no petty talk, no malice.

"You, who are comprehending, purify my heart."

At the physical level, we can understand that our heart must be purified in order to enjoy perfect health. But its meaning here is much deeper than that. The heart is the seat of consciousness. Accessing the wisdom of the heart connects you with the larger wisdom of our world and opens up the doorway into the heart of the universe. Once you make that connection, you begin to live in a way that is wise yet kind, practical yet spontaneous, courageous yet caring, responsible yet passionate. This means that every idea, every sensation, every action and expression of your life must be in balance. You must be 'purified' physically, mentally and spiritually before there can be right understanding. It takes effort and time to get the balance right.

There is a wonderful story told by our rishis. It was believed that every person was a god and because human beings abused their Divine power, God took that power away and He hid that great power – the source of all human talent, potential, magnificence and glory, in a place where they would least search. And that place is the 'spiritual heart'.

In these lessons, the importance is given to the 'spiritual heart'. When the rishis entered deep states of meditation, what they saw was a flame the size of the thumb – *angusht atman* – on the right side of their heart. This is a great experience, when a person becomes one with the universe and the face radiates light. After this experience, if one leads a pure and balanced life, he will reflect this radiance always. The light we see in the persona of sages is radiance that is reflected of the 'knowing' and experience of the 'oneness'. The right expression of life then depends on a heart that is purified. This means that every idea, every sensation, every action and expression of your life must be in balance.

Preparation for Meditation

"You, who are the cause of the universe, purify my body."

The body is a three-fold entity: physical, mental and spiritual. Your 'mind' is made up of ideas that come to you and which you hold for your own, the origin for which is the universal mind. Just as you see that every living thing is linked with the breath of life, so also in thought every living thing is linked together. Inculcate the idea of health of the body, joy of the mind and reverence of the spirit. This is the eternal triangle of life: joy, gratitude, reverence.

"You, who are all sustaining, purify my feet."

The feet are an important extension of the body. We would not be able to go far without our feet. But spiritually, the 'feet' form the contact between you and the earth upon which you stand. The magnetic pull of the earth upon which you stand, comes into the body through the contact made by the feet.

"You, who are all truth, purify again my head."

Through your 'head' comes understanding. May the understanding be right. This course has been designed to clear away the cobwebs surrounding man's consciousness so that he is able to discard the shackles of the conditioned mind, break away from tradition, and with courage and diligence work towards finding his true nature.

"You, who are all pervading, purify my whole organism."

If you have been diligent in your practice, then with the practise of 'Your Own Spiritual Breath' and its Affirmation, you will be able to experience what this means.

According to science, the universe came into existence with the 'big bang'. Thereafter, all life started i.e. unicellular, multicellular, reptiles, birds, mammals and human beings. In the evolutionary system, all are created for a Divine purpose.

'Purify my whole organism' refers to what is expected of you as a human being in reference to the mechanism of universal balancing. With the Affirmation of 'Your Own Spiritual Breath' you become one with the Universal Consciousness, and your love vibration reaches every living thing, from bacteria to micro organisms, and then comes back to you and you get lost in it and you are all, you are the universe. And then, you are only *ananda* or pure bliss.

'Organism' means this organ that has taken birth for a Divine purpose. Through the practise of the Breaths, the grossness drops away and the subtle body can expand as far as your imagination and feeling will go. With the Affirmation of 'Your Own Spiritual Breath' you are expanding and becoming one with all flora and fauna and everything that comes in contact with you. You will achieve this state of wholeness where you become one with all existence. Once this happens, then you will get the answer to "*Koham, Koham?*" or "Who am I?" You will realise that you are "*Soham*" or "I am That." This state is the state in meditation when you become one with God Consciousness.

This state can only be reached when there is extreme longing and yearning for the Divine. Once that has been achieved, the guidance for you comes from the God within you. Unless and until you practise as per the dictum only then the Source Consciousness starts to reveal itself to you slowly.

Chapter Twenty Two

Meditation

"When you rise to another dimension, you do so with the help of meditation. There is no other way to achieve spiritual awakening except through meditation. With the help of Kundalini you will experience various indications of awakening."

– Swami Rama

When one sits for meditation, one is advised to watch the breath. In Eckhart Tolle's words:

"The fact that breath has no form is one of the reasons why breath awareness is an extremely effective way of bringing space into your life, of generating consciousness. It is an excellent meditation object precisely because it is not an object, has no shape or form... Being aware of your breath forces you into the present moment – the key to all inner transformation."

The Eight Spiritual Breaths

When you sit for meditation and you are told to watch your breath and 'just relax', it somehow seems impossible. How can you relax when there is so much inner turmoil going on? It is at that very moment that thoughts from all over converge on your mind. But then, how can one achieve that state of relaxation? The nature of meditation is always non-doing. It is always passive and in order to achieve the state of non-doing, you have to do something. Therefore, meditation has two steps: the active and the passive.

Affirmations for meditation are given to you so that instead of the mind directing you into random activity, you direct it into guided and fruitful activity before it leads into quietude where everything ends. In that state you can be passive and meditation happens; then meditation 'is' and you are 'not'. Even if there is activity around you, there will be silence within you. Out of this silence, creativity will arise.

What happens in life is that the challenge is always new, but our response is old because it is formed on the past, which is memory. When we experience without past conditioning i.e. from traditions passed on to us by our forefathers, our experiencing is altogether different. A new thought or an inspiration can happen only when the mind is not caught in the net of memory.

After performing all the Eight Breathing Exercises and Affirmations, you should lie down flat without a pillow. Place your right hand over the left on your Manipur chakra (over the navel); right leg over the left and close your eyes. Breathe calmly and with perfect rhythm; imagine yourself as 'watching the breath'. This will give you a feeling of perfect poise and relaxation.

Start reciting the Meditational Affirmations and Negations given in the next chapter. If you have not memorised them, then you can record them in your own voice and listen to them with your eyes closed.

This will help clear old karmic data by bringing it to the surface.

Meditation

You need to just be a witness to whatever unfolds without getting involved in it. Affirm that you are health, strength, youth and beauty.

Observe this position for a couple of months. You may feel or sense data of stored memories coming up. Be a witness to whatever comes up. When no memories are coming up, you could then change the position of your hands to your chest i.e. on the Anahat chakra.

Give thanks to the Infinite Wisdom in which there is all knowledge, for the youth that is being made manifest in your body.

Chapter Twenty Three

Meditational Affirmations and Negations

"In the universal wheel of Time, the Ishwara, the Lord, the Master, causes the destined deeds of Karma to be performed. All beings revolve as though mounted on a potter's wheel. The Master is the Regulator, not blind Fate or Chance."

Bhagawad Gita – Swami Chinmayananda's commentary on the Hymn to Dakshinamoorthy by Sri Sankaracharya

Memorise and recite the following:

- I am now entering upon the greatest teaching accessible to man for I am learning the secret of existence.

- The riddle of the universe is about me; I am now solving it.

- I learn why men die, why they are born, and why they live.

- I learn why men succeed and why they fail, why they are happy and why they are discontented. I have the power and ability to live as long as I desire, to achieve whatever

Meditational Affirmations and Negations

  I wish and the doors of my mind are now open that I may learn how this is done.
- I now learn that man is the Master of his destiny, that man is the author of his death. I realise that death is a mental concept and not a law of life.
- I now realise that all negation is a mental concept and not a law of life.
- I learn that there is only one law of creation, the law of life.
- I am now developing the power and the ability to realise in my own life the one Divine principle in which all success, happiness and peace reside.
- **And I thank the Infinite Spirit within me for the knowledge of this wondrous truth now revealed to my consciousness.**

Denial:
- Death is not a law of life – man is not subject to decay, disease or old age – there is no old age – there is no decay – there is no death – there is no death.
- I am not subject to decay and old age – now I am free – free – free for evermore.

Affirmation:
- The law of creation is life, I am life – glorious, wondrous, vibrant life. I am youth. I am beauty, strength, power. I am free. Free life. Life. I am life – eternal, boundless, limitless, everlasting, never-ending, wonderful life... I am free... free... free!
- I am the Master of my own life... I will do whatever I desire to do... I rejoice! I did not feel this before, but now I know it. I feel with all the power of my being that I am the Master of my own life, and I will begin now to truly live it.

The Eight Spiritual Breaths

- I am now developing creative wisdom through my imagination. I am a channel of creative wisdom. Creative wisdom is the light of my mind. I am free from all negation.

- I am whole. I am perfect. I am strong. I am powerful. I am loving. I am harmonious. I am rich. I am young. I am happy.

- The Creator is right here, right here in the heart of me, right here in the mind of me, right here in the being of me, right here in the substance of me... making Itself known, reveal Thyself, O Lord of my life. O Lord of the eternal. That in which I live and move and have my being. Come!.. I wait... I listen... I am still, I look within me... Come!

- From now on and forever, I, the creative spirit, differentiated from all other life forms, embody myself in perfect health, beauty and strength. I am imperishable... I am indivisible... I am exhaustless.

- I am the creative spirit embodied... I am life eternal. I am in eternity now – right here. I am Eternal now – right now. I am eternal life – I am life eternal.

- You, O Lord, who are the life and support of the universe, who are dearer than life, purify my head.

    You, who are free from all pain, by coming into contact with whom I am free from all troubles, purify my eyes.

    You, who pervade the universe, directing and controlling it, purify my throat.

    You, who are comprehending, purify my heart.

    You, who are the cause of the universe, purify my body.

    You, who are all-sustaining, purify my feet.

    You, who are all-truth, purify again my head.

    You, who are all-pervading, purify my whole organism.

Meditational Affirmations and Negations

Denial:
- I am not separate from the universe.

Affirmation:
- I am the centre of attraction. I am a magnet.
- I embody myself in youth and beauty. I embody myself in the substance of beauty.

Denial:
- Death is not a principle in nature.

Affirmation:
- I am life. I am the creative spirit, radiant, beautiful, strong, glorious, animate, energy, force, life, eternal life.
- I and the Creator are one. I am the creative spirit. I am immortal.
- I am Imperishable. I am self-existent. I am all-pervading.
- I am established in strength, beauty, health and joy.
- I am youth... radiant... beautiful... I am eternally young.
- I am strong... eternal life... youth... beauty... I am free... free... free...
- I rejoice, I am glad that there is no old age – I am not subject to old age – I am free... free... free... free forever.

Denial:
- I am not subject to decay, disease, old age, senility.

Affirmation:
- I am young, I am eternally young... I am eternal life – life, health, beauty, joy and truth... youth, youth, youth.

Chapter Twenty Four

Awakening

Under the guidance of the guru, the Brahma Vidya course led to my 'awakening'. This means, it led me to a new way of thinking. This 'awakening' just happens. There is nothing you can do to awaken; the reason being that you are clueless as to what the word means. It has to happen. How it happens or what form it takes will be unique to you.

How does the course of Brahma Vidya help you then? It helps by clearing out your old data of preconceived notions, freeing you from individual and collective belief systems and by throwing out toxins clogging your mental and emotional bodies. This in turn allows new knowledge and understanding to filter in, which is easily assimilated. The practise of this course helps you understand that awareness is the light that enters the darkness and frees you from your illusions. It helps you to move towards your 'awakening' in a systematic and organised manner. The realisation dawns that you are the sole source of your own creation, and so you open yourself to the possibility of experiencing oneness, the rediscovery of what you are.

Until this happens, you continue in your dream state moving on the wheel of your karma, continually repeating yourself over and over again in different lifetimes, reacting and responding from a set of existing conditioning and belief systems stored in your memory bank.

Awakening

Life moving on the wheel of karma.

As one experiences the world, or to be more precise, as one experiences life, one feels that the whole world is going through the same experience.

That is the way I felt during the process of my awakening. I had to undergo a process that was mainly related to the chakras through which a new state of consciousness gradually awakened, transforming my way of thinking and being, and becoming integrated into my life over a period of nearly eight years. It is a shift in consciousness in which thinking and awareness separate; awareness becomes conscious of its involvement or un-involvement with a particular thought or situation. You become alert to your thought and instead of getting entangled in it, with awareness you can control it. The questioning is now coupled with the understanding of the wisdom given to us by wise men of yore, hidden in the depths of the belief system, mythological stories and the symbols.

The ancients devised different means of imparting this knowledge, keeping in mind the development of consciousness at different levels of human existence. Those who had evolved from the devotion and worship of a personal god, cleared and re-scripted the grooves of their brain through *mantra* recitation and could relate to a Formless Reality. They were given the teachings of *Advaita* or One Source Consciousness. Those with a less developed consciousness were given knowledge in the form of stories; and those with a denser consciousness were given strict rules and fear-based belief systems to gradually mould their consciousness.

The time has come when their foresight has proved fruitful. No longer are individuals adhering to old beliefs and stories blindly. Their questioning is now coupled with a new understanding, thus experiencing within themselves the breaking of mind patterns based on the individual self or the ego.

The newly found ability of rising above thought and realising a dimension within ourselves that is beyond thought, allows us to no longer derive our identity from thoughts or from our belief system and conditioned behaviour patterns of the collective consciousness. The understanding dawns that the – "I, I, I" that goes on is really not "Who I am." The question then arises, "Who am I?" The answer comes, "I am the awareness that is aware and knows that a thought has arisen." And when in this awareness any thought, emotion or action arises, it is also dealt with awareness and understanding. A reaction then becomes a response and anger becomes an understanding. The 'awareness' is in the background as the 'observer'. When that happens, you are free from the unobserved mind and then every thought, word and action is a conscious happening in full awareness of the result and the consequences. It is then that the true meaning of peace and happiness is realised.

Once we have reached this level of consciousness, we then consciously decide what kind of relationship we want to have with the present moment. Once we have decided what we want the present moment to be, we then make the first move and soon we will see the results. Life becomes friendly towards us, people become more helpful and circumstances more cooperative. One decision taken in awareness changes our reality.

Books of Reference

A New Earth – Eckhart Tolle

Brahma Vidya – Initiate Group Course – Swami K. S. Ramanathan

Breath of Life – Edwin J. Dingle

Concentration and Meditation – Swami Sivananda

I Can Do It – Louise L. Hay

Kundalini, Evolution and Enlightenment – John White

Kundalini Tantra – Swami Satyananda Saraswati

Master Charles – Inner Network Newsletter, Synchronicity Foundation

Meditation and Its Practice – Swami Rama

Meditation: The Art of Ecstasy – Osho

My Life in Tibet – Ding Le Mei

Nawa Yogini Tantra, Yoga for Women – Swami Muktananda

Prana Pranayama Prana Vidya – Swami Niranjanananda Saraswati

The Chakras – C. W. Leadbeater

The Chakras and Esoteric Healing – Zachary F. Landsdowne, Ph.D

The Miracle of the Breath – Andy Caponigro

The Monk Who Sold His Ferrari – Robin Sharma

The Saint, The Surfer and The CEO – Robin Sharma

The Second Dawn: Revival of Shaktipat Knowledge – Swami Shivom Tirth

Illustrations taken from *The Kundalini Trilogy* – Santosh Sachdev, are reproduced here in black and white. For actual colour illustrations, you will need to refer to the books in *The Kundalini Trilogy*.

Glossary

Brahma Vidya Knowledge of the Self.

Brahman The supreme experience of Godhood, the Impersonal Absolute God.

chakra Wheel or disc; in yogic literature, one of the several centres of consciousness located in the etheric body, usually depicted as a lotus flower.

Hanuman Vaanara God of Strength and Wisdom, chief devotee of Ram.

Ida One of the two main channels (lunar and left) within the body through which the Kundalini ascends.

karma Based on the principle of reincarnation, the system of Divine Justice whereby people face the results of their positive and negative thoughts and actions.

karmic Pertaining to karma and its unfolding.

Kundalini The manifestation of the Dynamic Female Cosmic Energy within the individual body, lying nascent in a coiled form at the base of the spine.

Maha Tattva Main Tattva (element).

Mahaprana Main Prana (life force).

mantra Sacred chant, constituting a precise arrangement of syllables with a particular occult significance, especially empowered by the application of the Aum. The science of mantras derives from the knowledge of the subtle yet transformative influence of thought, power and sound frequencies in the etheric or astral dimensions.

Glossary

nada Sound, usually implying a haunting resonance.

nadi Etheric channel for energy flow within the body. Out of a total of 72,000 nadis in a human body, there are 100 major ones. Among these, there are three main nadis, including the pingala, or the solar nadi, on the right side of the spinal column; ida, or the lunar nadi, located on the left side; and the most important one of all, the central nadi, called the sushumna, vehicle of the balanced energy flow indicative of spiritual growth.

Pingala One of the two main channels (solar and right) within the body through which the Kundalini ascends.

Prana The Life Force or vital energy, which constitutes the breath in living beings.

Pranayama The breath control exercises of yoga to gain mastery over the Prana.

Pranic Pertaining to Prana.

sadhana Adoption of meditation, asceticism and devotional practices on the spiritual path.

Shiva One of the Hindu Trinity, the Androgynous God of Destruction.

Shiva mantra Om Namah Shivaya, the basic mantra used by the devotees of Lord Shiva.

Sushumana The nadi, or energy channel, that leads to the Sacral chakra, the sushumana.

Tantric One who practices Tantra, pertaining to tantra.

Tattva Literally, 'basic stuff', i.e. element.

For information on Santosh Sachdeva, visit:
www.santoshsachdeva.com

The author may be contacted on email:
mails@santoshsachdeva.com

For further details, contact:
Yogi Impressions Books Pvt. Ltd.
1711, Centre 1, World Trade Centre,
Cuffe Parade, Mumbai 400 005, India.

Fill in the Mailing List form on our website and receive, via email, information on books, authors, events and more.
Visit: www.yogiimpressions.com

Telephone: (022) 61541500, 61541541
Fax: (022) 61541542
E-mail: yogi@yogiimpressions.com

Join us on Facebook:
www.facebook.com/yogiimpressions

Lightning Source UK Ltd.
Milton Keynes UK
UKOW03f2234100314

227916UK00001B/53/P